D0467726

fabric
Scrapping

fabric

Katie Ebben

Scrapping

STERLING

New York / London
www.sterlingpublishing.com

photography by Chris Tubbs

First published in 2008 by
Jacqui Small LLP
An imprint of Aurum Press Ltd
7 Greenland Street
London NW1 0ND

First published in the U.S. in 2008 by
Sterling Publishing Co., Inc.
387 Park Avenue South
New York, NY 10016

Distributed in Canada by Sterling Publishing
c/o Canadian Manda Group, 165 Dufferin Street,
Toronto, Ontario, Canada M6K 3HG

Text and projects copyright © Katie Ebben 2008

Photography, design and layout copyright
© Jacqui Small 2008

The author's moral rights have been asserted.

All rights reserved. No part of this book may
be reproduced, stored in a retrieval system or
transmitted, in any form or by any means,
electronic, electrostatic, magnetic tape,
mechanical, photocopying, recording or
otherwise, without prior permission in writing
from the publisher.

Publisher **Jacqui Small**
Editorial Manager **Judith Hannam**
Commissioning Editor **Zia Mattocks**
Art Director **Maggie Town**
Designer **Beverly Price**
Photographer **Chris Tubbs**
Stylist **Katie Ebben**
Production **Peter Colley**

ISBN-13: 978-1-4027-4867-7
ISBN-10: 1-4027-4867-1

Library of Congress Cataloging-in-Publication
Data Available

10 9 8 7 6 5 4 3 2 1

Printed in Singapore

For information about custom editions, special sales,
premium and corporate purchases, please contact
Sterling Special Sales Department at
800-805-5489 or specialsales@sterlingpublishing.com.

Contents

Introduction

Quite when or how my passion for fabric started I'm not entirely sure, but for as far back as I can remember I've had a sewing box of some description, packed with mismatching fabric scraps, embroidery thread, buttons, needles, and pins that were too precious to throw away. I'd happily spend hours just arranging all the bits and pieces in my red-and-white cane sewing basket, which had gathered pockets around the sides and padding on the interior of the lid that doubled as a pincushion. Ahhh, happy days!

If you're also an avid hoarder of fabric and all the associated items that "will come in useful one day," then this book is for you. I didn't have to travel far for inspiration, I merely had a long look—or should I say rummage—inside the overflowing boxes and overstuffed suitcases stacked in my workroom, made a big mess and sat down in the middle of it all thinking about what I could make.

So this book is all about using up what you've got in order to make something stylish and useful, having a go and a bit of fun while you're at it— otherwise, what's the point? There's also the added reward of clearing some space and relieving the guilt of making new acquisitions. The projects are all 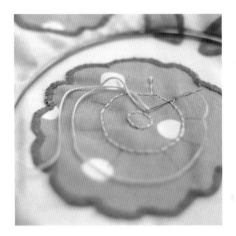 very straightforward; none of them involves complicated techniques and while some are super-quick to make, others will take longer. Save those up for the winter when you're more inclined to stay indoors and stitch away while watching reruns of your favorite TV show.

Each of the five chapters covers different sewing techniques and offers lots of creative ideas for using up fabric remnants. The first, "Use it up," is filled with simple but effective ways to make use of all those really small scraps, ranging from pretty mix 'n' match napkins to festive strings of bunting. The third and fourth chapters, "Cover it up" and "Mix it up," explore the traditional techniques of appliqué and patchwork interpreted in a modern way. These projects are also ideal for using up small scraps but they vary in scale, so if you're new to either technique, start with something small like the floral appliqué cushion (page 70) or the personalized patched cushion (page 92) before venturing on to more ambitious designs, such as the appliqué chair cover (page 78) or

the quilted patchwork bedspread (page 102). You may have to buy the odd item to complete a project, such as batting for the bedspread or tarp backing for the waterproof picnic rug (page 112), but the bulk of most of the projects can easily be made from small bits and pieces of fabric.

As well as explaining how to make items from scratch, a selection of projects in the second chapter, "Sew it on," show how to customize bought items, such as bedlinen, scatter cushions, towels and curtains, breathing new life and charm into them with a more personalized and embellished look. The fifth chapter, "Make it new," is all about reinvention and includes a bolster cover made from a vintage silk scarf (page 122) and a laundry bag made by stitching together a collection of linen tea towels (page 134).

Alongside the projects are helpful tips and additional practical ideas that I hope will inspire you to use up all those bits and pieces that might otherwise never see the light of day.

All the projects included in this book were made from real scraps of material—I didn't go out and buy yards of new fabric—so some of the step-by-step photographs show slightly different fabrics or sections of fabric from the ones used for the finished item, and it's this that makes the book authentic. When you are making your own items, don't try to find an exact replica of the fabrics I've used; instead, work with what you've got—after all, that's the whole point of fabric scrapping.

Sourcing fabric

Keep your eyes peeled and your mind open when hunting for fabric. The most obvious sources are department stores, where fabric is sold on the roll, but my favorite places to look are junk stores and charity stores. Don't expect to find fabric on a roll here, though you may; instead, look for drapes, bedlinen, table linen and clothing, which can be cut up and made into something else. These stores often have boxes of odd buttons, zippers, thread, wool, needles, lace, and braid, too, so ask if you

can't find any. And if you're buying lots of items, remember to haggle.

Local auction rooms—those that specialize in house clearances rather than the ones that sell priceless antiques—are great places to source fabric. Check out box lots and look for items such as samplers or needlepoint pictures that could be made into cushion covers or bags.

The Internet is probably the best place to pick up retro fabrics and auction sites such as eBay are an obvious hunting ground for bargains. Collectable fabrics, especially those dating from the Fifties, Sixties, and Seventies, can be expensive, so always check the provenance—if fabric is reproduction rather than original it should (but won't always) be cheaper.

Lastly, before you embark on a shopping spree, look around your home and those of obliging relatives for covetable scraps. Attics and closets are often rewarding spots for unearthing fabric treasures.

Selecting fabric

When you're surveying your stash of fabric and deciding which pieces to use for each project, bear the following points in mind.

❀ The weight of a fabric will, on the whole, determine what it is suitable for. Gauzy muslin is fine for hanging at windows, but is too delicate to use for making cushion covers as it won't withstand daily wear and tear. Similarly, denim cotton is great for upholstery and loose covers, but is less suited to making a patchwork quilt as it is thick and hard to sew when cut into small pieces.

❀ Check the cut edges of a fabric to see how easily it frays. If it does fray easily, you will need to finish the edges with zigzag stitch to prevent seams from falling apart with use.

❀ Is your fabric wide enough for the intended project?

❀ Is it washable and will it shrink? If so, wash and iron the fabric before cutting out the pieces you need.

❀ Check for flaws and stains—if the fabric is marked, can you work around it?

❀ When buying vintage fabric, check for fading; this tends to affect items such as bedspreads and drapes in particular.

❀ If you are buying vintage fabric, check that it's authentic. Is the design matched with the type of fabric that was used in that era? For example, bark cloth, a fabric with a slubby weave, was hugely popular in the Fifties, as were rayon and acetate.

Sewing-box basics

Below is a list of all the bits and pieces of equipment you will need, alongside a sewing machine, to complete the projects in this book.

Dressmaking scissors
These have long blades for cutting fabric; keep them sharp by only ever using them for cutting fabric. (A separate pair of scissors for cutting paper patterns and templates are useful to have, too.)

Pinking shears
Scissors with serrated edges that prevent cut edges from fraying.

Tape measure
This is essential for accuracy. Always smooth fabric out on a flat, firm surface before measuring it and cutting out patterns.

Needles
Keep spare needles for your sewing machine as well as a selection in various lengths and thicknesses for hand-sewing. The finer the fabric, the thinner the needle you should use and vice versa for thicker cloth.

Pins
As for needles, the finer the fabric, the finer the pins need to be.

Tacking thread
Thread that breaks readily, so it is easy to remove from finished sewing.

Sewing thread
Match your sewing thread to your fabric—for example, cotton thread with cotton cloth; polyester thread with mixed-fiber fabrics, and so on.

Fabric pen
Handy for marking patterns and sewing lines on fabric, fabric pens are either washable (you remove the pen marks with a damp cloth or wash the fabric) or they fade within a period of time.

Thimble
Useful to help push pins through stiff or thick fabric and to protect your fingers from needle pricks when hand-sewing—wear it on the middle finger of your sewing hand.

Unpicker or seam ripper
This has a hooked end with a tiny blade and is useful for unpicking stitches and making buttonholes.

Pincushion
Useful for holding pins and needles as you sew, some pincushions can be attached to your wrist.

Safety pins
Useful for threading ribbon or cord through a stitched drawstring channel and for holding thick layers of fabric together when quilting.

Use it up

If, like me, you have a suitcase full of "it might come in useful for something" bits and pieces of fabric, then this chapter is for you. The most important rules when using up scraps are to choose materials of a similar weight and fiber content, which makes them easier to work with and helps ensure a successful end result, and to mix colors and patterns that blend well together. Look at paint charts or soft-furnishing brochures for inspiration on how to combine colors, patterns, and textures.

A mixture of practical everyday items and great gifts for friends and family, the following projects are quick to make and a good starting point for less experienced sewers. For example, the party bunting on page 38 is very simple and will help build up confidence in using a sewing machine, while the floral tiebacks on page 26 involve just a little hand-sewing and provide a can't-go-wrong introduction to freehand machine embroidery.

Frilled peg bag

This is a sweet way of using up lots of different strips of fabric in an array of patterns—just choose a unifying color theme to pull it all together. I have decorated only the front of the peg bag with frills and used a contrasting fabric for the back, but you can add frills to the back, too, if you wish—simply cut out double the number of strips and attach them in the same way as for the front of the bag.

Materials

16 x 12 in. (40 x 30 cm) of fabric for the back of the bag

6 x 12 in. (15.5 x 30 cm) of fabric for the top front of the bag

10 x 12 in. (25.5 x 30 cm) of fabric for the bottom front of the bag

3 strips of fabric 3½ x 12 in. (9 x 30 cm) for the flat frills

5 strips of fabric 3½ x 22 in. (9 x 55 cm) for the ruched frills

Baby's clothes hanger

Tape measure

Dressmaking scissors or pinking shears

Pins

Sewing thread

Sewing machine

Iron and ironing board

Needle

Pencil or fabric pen

Embroidery thread

1 Cut out the fabric pieces—one back piece, two front pieces, three strips for the flat frills, and five longer strips for the ruched frills.

Hem all the strips of fabric for the flat and ruched frills. To do this, turn the edges over to the wrong side of the fabric by approximately ¼ in. (0.5 cm), pin in place and machine stitch, then press to give neat edges.

1

2 To make the ruched fills, using a needle and thread, sew running stitch by hand (see pages 88–9) along the top edge of one of the longer strips. Gently pull one end of the thread to ruche the material until it measures 11½ in. (29 cm) along the gathered edge, then secure the thread with a couple of knots. Repeat to make four more ruched frills.

3 Take the two pieces of fabric that will make up the front of the bag. Hem the bottom 12 in. (30 cm) edge of the top piece and the top 12 in. (30 cm) edge of the bottom piece to make a neat opening. To do this, turn the edges under by ¼ in. (0.5cm), pin, then machine stitch.

To attach the frills, place one frill on the right side of the bottom piece of the bag front, 3 in. (8 cm) up from the bottom edge. Pin in place along the top edge of the frill, then machine stitch. Attach the next frill above the first so that it overlaps by 1¼ in. (3 cm), pin it in place along the top edge of the frill, then machine stitch as before. Repeat for all the frills, randomly interspersing flat frills with ruched frills as you wish.

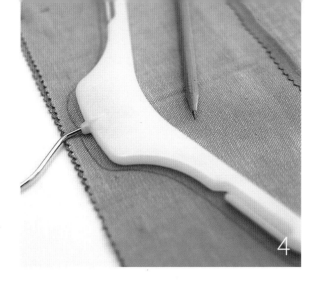

4

4 Take the back piece of the bag and the top piece of the bag front. Place them with right sides together and pin along the top edge.

 To make the hanger shape at the top of the bag, lay the hanger in position on the back piece of the bag and draw along the top edge of the hanger using a pencil or fabric pen.

5

5 Pin ⅝ in. (1.5 cm) above this line to create a seam allowance, then cut along the pinned line. Tack along the drawn line, then machine stitch, leaving a ¼ in. (0.5 cm) gap in the middle of the seam for the hanger to slide through. Remove the tacking and press the seams open.

6 To assemble the bag, pin the bottom piece of the bag front to the back piece of the bag, with right sides together and allowing a ⅝ in. (1.5 cm) seam. Make sure that the edges of the two front pieces just overlap at the opening, then pin the sides of the top piece of the bag front to the back piece, with a ⅝ in. (1.5 cm) seam allowance as before. Machine stitch the sides and bottom edge of the bag, taking care not to trap the edges of the frills in the stitching. Press the seams open and turn the bag right sides out.

 Work blanket stitch (see pages 88–9) along the lower edge of the bag opening using a needle and six strands of embroidery thread.

 Slide the hook of the hanger through the hole in the top of the bag and fill with pegs.

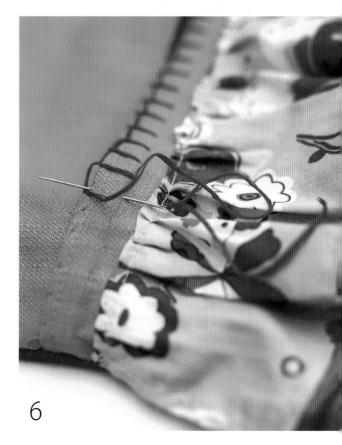

6

Animal friends

Great gifts for grown-ups as well as children, these cute fabric animals are a good way of using up small odds and ends of material. Add a handful of lavender to the stuffing and attach a length of ribbon to make a fragrant sachet to hang in your wardrobe, or arrange them in groups on a shelf to create a menagerie.

Materials

8 x 16 in. (20 x 40 cm) of fabric for each animal

Animal templates

Fabric pen

Pinking shears

Needle

Embroidery thread

8–12 in. (20–30 cm) of ¼ in.- (5 mm-) wide ribbon for each animal (see step 3), and/or silk flowers for decoration

Sewing thread

Pins

Tacking thread

Sewing machine

Batting

TRACE OFF THE TEMPLATE OF YOUR CHOICE, SHOWN HERE AT ACTUAL SIZE, OR ENLARGE TO MAKE BIGGER TOYS

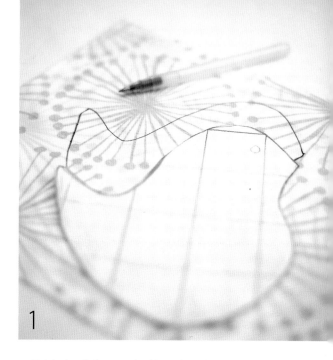

1 Fold the fabric in half with right sides together. Trace around your chosen template with a fabric pen and use pinking shears to cut out the animal shape.

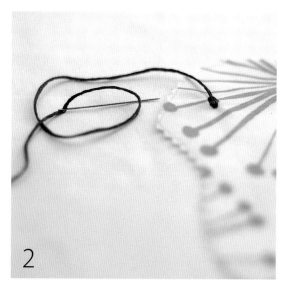

2 Draw a circle for the eyes on the right side of each fabric shape with the fabric pen. Using a needle and four strands of embroidery thread, sew the eyes with long stitches laid side by side.

3 To make the head and tail feathers for the bird, and the tail and mane for the donkey, cut two pieces of ribbon to length—about 4 in. (10 cm) for the bird's head and tail feathers and 8 in. (20 cm) for the donkey's mane and tail. For the bird's feathers, make three loops and secure the ends with a couple of stitches; for the donkey's tail, make two loops and secure the ends with a couple of stitches; for the mane, make six small loops and secure as before.

Place the two pieces of fabric with right sides together and position the ribbon loops between them with the cut ends of the ribbon aligned with the edges of the fabric and the loops pointing inward; pin in place.

4 Continue pinning all around the edges of the fabric pieces with a 1/4 in. (0.5 cm) seam allowance, then tack, leaving a 1 1/4 in. (3 cm) gap at the bottom of the animal to allow you to turn the fabric right sides out. Sew on the sewing machine using running stitch, then remove the tacking, trim the seams and press them open. Turn the fabric right sides out and stuff the animal with batting. Close the opening at the bottom with slip stitch (see step 2 on page 60).

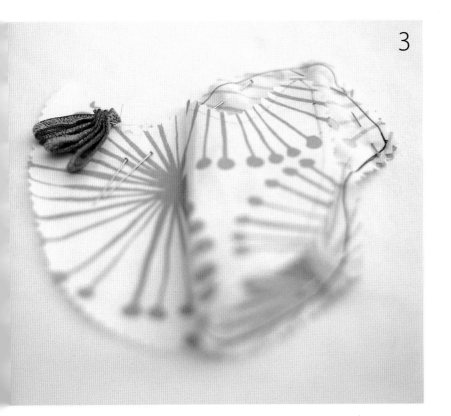

Tips

✂ You can use more ribbon, embroidery thread, and silk flowers to add extra decoration to your animal (as shown on the pink bird).

✂ If you are giving the toy to a baby or young child, make sure there is nothing small, such as buttons or beads, that could be pulled off and choked on.

Floral tiebacks

There are a lot of uses for these pretty flower corsages, so there's no need to limit them to curtain tiebacks. Attach a safety pin to the back (instead of wire) and use them to decorate a shopping bag or the lapel of a jacket. You could even attach them to a hair band to give a ponytail a girlie touch. Alternatively, brighten up your sofa by sewing them onto plain cushions.

Materials

8 x 8 in. (20 x 20 cm) of pink-patterned fabric

8 x 8 in. (20 x 20 cm) of felt, in bright pink, pale pink, and white

8 x 8 in. (20 x 20 cm) of white or cream organza

4 x 86½ in. (10 x 220 cm) of pink-patterned fabric for the tieback

Flower templates

Pencil or fabric pen

8 x 8 in. (20 x 20 cm) of iron-on interfacing

Iron and ironing board

White sewing thread

Sewing machine

Dressmaking scissors

Needle

Yellow and black embroidery thread

Florist's wire

Fabric glue

Twenty ½ in. (18 mm) beads

BACK

MIDDLE

TOP

BOTTOM

TRACE OFF THE TEMPLATES,
SHOWN HERE AT ACTUAL SIZE

2 Using the second-largest template, trace and cut out one pale pink, one bright pink, and one white felt flower. Using the smallest template, cut out three white felt flowers—these will be used on the back of the corsages later. As before, and using the remaining template, trace and cut out three organza flowers.

1

2

1 Using the largest template and a pencil or fabric pen, draw three flowers for each tieback onto the patterned fabric. Then, following the manufacturer's instructions, attach the iron-on interfacing to the back of the fabric.

Using the freehand embroidery foot on your sewing machine and white thread, loosely trace the shape of the petals with running stitch, sewing just inside the drawn line. Don't worry if the fabric wrinkles slightly or if your stitching is a bit wobbly.

Cut out the flowers with sharp scissors, cutting outside the line of stitching, but inside the drawn line.

3 Using a needle and four strands of yellow embroidery thread, decorate the three medium-sized felt flowers with running stitch (see pages 88–9). Start in the center and sew three lines down each petal.

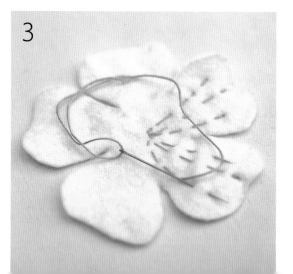

3

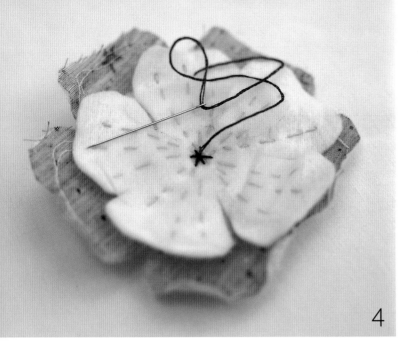

4

4 To assemble each corsage, lay one decorated felt flower on top of one large patterned-fabric flower and then place one organza flower on top. Using black embroidery thread, sew all three petals together, making a small star shape in the center of the flower.

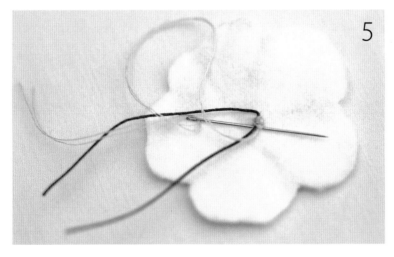

5

5 Cut a 4-in. (10-cm) length of florist's wire and fold it in half. Using a needle and thread, attach the wire to the center of the smallest white felt flower. Using fabric glue, attach this flower to the back of the corsage for extra support.

6 To make the tieback, fold the 4 x 86½ in. (10 x 220 cm) strip of fabric in half lengthwise with right sides together. Pin at one end and along the length. Allowing a ½ in. (1 cm) seam, machine stitch, leaving the other end unsewn. Press the seams and turn right sides out.

Tie a knot 6 in. (15 cm) from the sewn end. Slide a bead into the open end of the fabric tube, and push it down to the knot. Bunch the fabric around the bead and tie a knot above it. Slide in another bead, tie a knot above it, and repeat until you have used all the beads. Finish with a knot, remembering to leave the last 6 in. (15 cm) of the fabric tube empty to match the other end of the tieback.

Turn in the open edges of the fabric and close with slip stitch (see step 2 on page 60).

Tie the tieback around a curtain and then attach the corsages to it, twisting the ends of the wires together on the inside to secure.

6

Mix 'n' match napkins

These napkins are lovely for informal lunches, tea time, or alfresco dining. Each one is made up of three different strips of fabric—use cotton or linen cast-offs for the best results. There are lots of ways in which you could personalize these napkins: for example, the corners can be monogrammed with initials, or you could make the napkins in festive shades for your Christmas table.

Materials

For each napkin: 3 strips of fabric 6 x 16½ in. (14.5 x 42 cm)

Pins

Needle

Tacking thread

Sewing machine

Sewing thread

Dressmaking scissors

Iron and ironing board

Small seed beads

Embroidery thread

1 The sections of the napkin are joined together with French seams so that all the raw edges are hidden. Place two strips of fabric with wrong sides together and pin, then tack a line close to the seam line, ⅝ in. (1.5 cm) in from the raw edge. Using the sewing machine, stitch a line ¼ in. (6 mm) away from the line of tacking (stitch this line within the seam allowance, not on the body of the fabric). Trim the fabric to within ⅛ in. (3 mm) of the stitched line, remove the tacking, and press the fabric open.

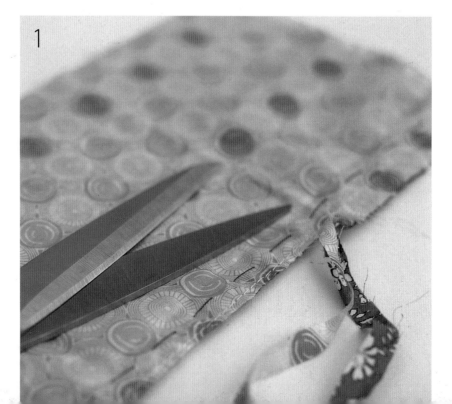

2 The next step is to encase the seam you have just sewn so that the raw edges are enclosed. Turn the fabric right sides together, fold along the line of stitching, and press flat.

Pin and tack the fabric to hold it in place, then stitch along the tacked line. Press the fabric and remove the tacking thread.

Repeat this process from step 1 to join the third piece of fabric.

3 Next, hem the napkin. Turn one edge of the napkin under by ¼ in. (7 mm), fold it over itself again, and pin. Repeat for all four sides, trimming the corners so that they lie flat. Topstitch the hem on the machine and press.

4 To stitch the floret in the corner of the napkin, thread the needle with three strands of embroidery thread and bring the needle and thread through to the front of the fabric in the center of where your floret will lie. Pull the needle through and reinsert it adjacent to the first entry point. Without pulling the needle through, bring it up through the fabric again between ¼–½ in. (5–10 mm) away; loop the thread under the tip of the needle and pull through. Reinsert the needle in the center of the floret (you are making a small circle that is the center of the flower) and repeat the previous step. Continue stitching until you have gone full circle, then secure on the back.

5 Attach a string of beads in a circle around the edge of the embroidered floret. To do this, thread the needle with three strands of embroidery thread and secure the end well but neatly on the back of the napkin, then bring the needle up from the back through to the front of the fabric. Thread enough beads onto the thread to lie in a circle around the floret and secure the end with a few stitches next to where you started. Do not cut the thread. Holding the beads in position, use the needle and thread to secure the beads in place. To do this, bring the needle up through the fabric close to a bead and pull it back through the fabric on the other side of the same bead. This creates a loop over the thread that the beads are strung on, which will hold them in place. Repeat around the entire circle of beads.

5

Scented sachets

These pretty sachets are quick and easy to make. Fill them with either buckwheat, which helps promote relaxation and sleep, or lavender, which is also a natural moth repellent and so protects linen as well as making it smell heavenly.

Materials

For the lavender sachets:

2 pieces of fabric 4½ x 4½ in. (11 x 11 cm)

2 pieces of fabric 2¾ x 2¾ in. (7 x 7 cm)

2 handfuls of lavender

20 in. (50 cm) of rickrack

For the buckwheat pillow:

10¼ x 9½ in. (26 x 24 cm) of fabric

5½ x 9½ in. (14 x 24 cm) of fabric

5 handfuls of buckwheat

20 in. (50cm) of ⅝ in.- (15mm-) wide ribbon

For both:

Dressmaking scissors

Pins

Sewing thread

Sewing machine

Iron and ironing board

Funnel or piece of paper

Needle

Lavender sachets

1 Cut the fabric to size. Pin the two larger squares together with right sides facing and a ½ in. (1 cm) seam allowance. Machine stitch all the way along three edges and three-quarters of the way along the fourth edge. Repeat for the two smaller squares. Press all the seams open and turn the sachets right sides out.

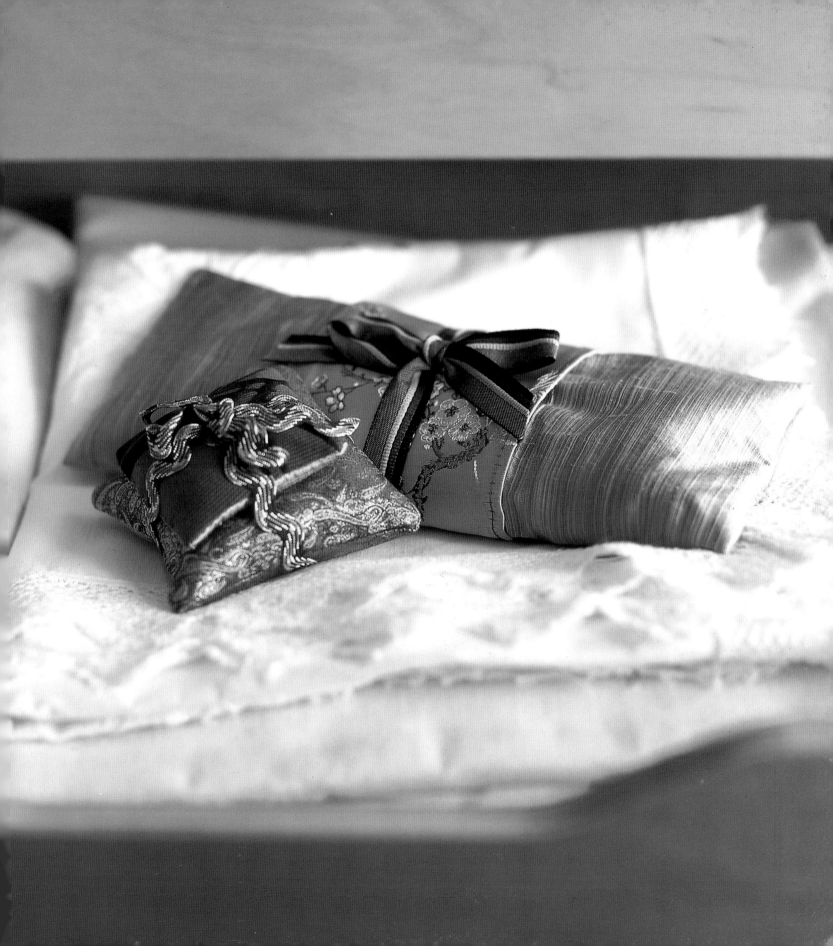

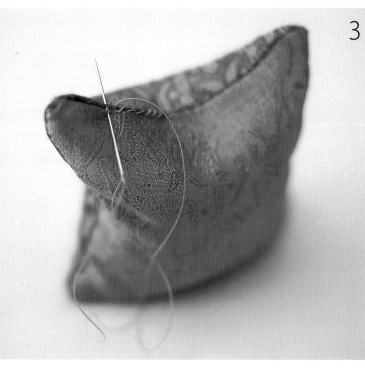

2 Using a funnel, or a piece of paper rolled into a funnel shape, fill the sachets with fresh lavender.

3 Turn in the seam allowance at the opening and pin, then use a needle and thread to close with slip stitch (see step 2 on page 60).

4 Stack the small pillow on top of the larger pillow and hold them in place using the length of rickrack tied in a bow.

Tip

✄ If the lavender scent starts to fade, refresh it with a few drops of lavender essential oil.

Buckwheat pillow

1 Fold the 10¼ x 9½ in. (26 x 24 cm) piece of fabric in half lengthwise with right sides facing. Pin then machine stitch along the longest edge, allowing a ½ in. (1 cm) seam. Press the seam open. Before sewing the sides together, position the seam centrally on the underside of the pillow. Pin the sides, then machine stitch all along one side and most of the way along the other, leaving a gap at one end through which to turn the pillow right sides out.

Press the seams open and turn right sides out. Using a funnel as before, fill the pillow with buckwheat. Turn the edges of the opening in, pin together and close with slip stitch.

1

2 To make the silk wrap for the pillow, take the piece of fabric measuring 5½ x 9½ in. (14 x 24 cm) and turn the two longest edges under by ¼ in. (0.5 cm), then again by ¼ in. (0.5 cm), to conceal the raw edges. Pin and machine stitch.

With right sides facing, fold the fabric in half; pin then machine stitch the short ends together, allowing a ½ in. (1 cm) seam. Press the seam open and turn the wrap right side out.

3 Slide the wrap onto the pillow and finish with the length of ribbon tied in a bow.

3

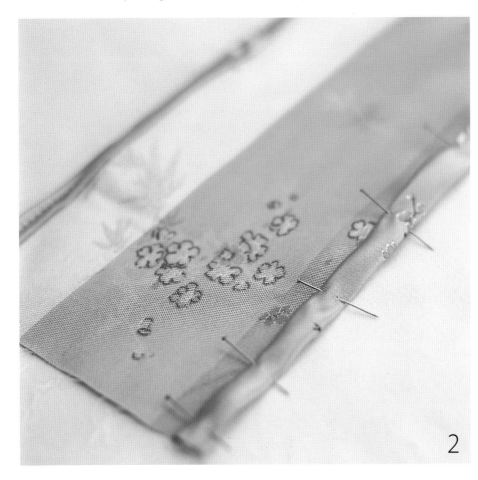

2

Party bunting

Bunting is very simple to make and ideal for using up odd scraps of fabric. Make pretty multicolored strings to hang between trees to add a festive touch to a summer garden party, or make it in white linen and organza to decorate a wedding tent. Bunting can be used indoors, too: you could add letters to each triangle of fabric to spell out a child's name and hang it above their bed, or even spell out the entire alphabet, if you have the time.

Materials

3 or more different fabrics

Triangle template made from card 7½ in. (19 cm) (top edge) x 8 in. (20 cm) (long edges)—including seam allowance

Pencil or fabric pen

Dressmaking scissors

Pins

Sewing thread

Sewing machine

Iron and ironing board

Artist's paintbrush

5½ yards (5 m) of ½ in.-(10 mm-) wide tape

Tape measure

1

1 Fold the fabric in half with right sides together (so it is doubled up) and trace around the triangle template with a pencil or fabric pen. Then cut out the triangle shapes using dressmaking scissors.

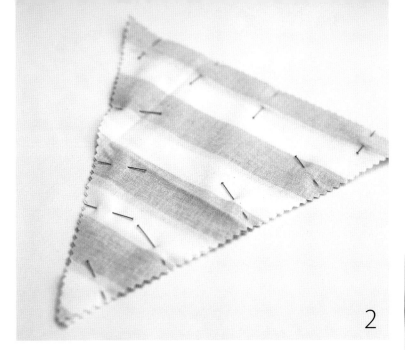

2

✿ Make different-sized flags to vary the pace, alternating between small, medium, and large.

✿ Play around with the gaps between the flags, too—but remember that the smaller the gap, the more flags you will have to make.

3

2 Allowing a ½ in. (1 cm) seam, pin along the edges of the triangles, joining the two layers of fabric together with right sides facing.

3 Machine stitch along the two long edges and part of the way along the top (shortest) edge, leaving a 1¾ in. (4 cm) gap to turn the triangles right sides out. Trim the seams and press them open, then turn the triangles right sides out. Use the end of an artist's paintbrush to push out the tips of the triangles.

4 Turn the seam allowance in on both sides of the opening and pin together. Press the flags flat. Lay the tape flat on a table and pin the top edge of the first flag to it, positioning it 12 in. (30 cm) from the end of the tape to allow sufficient free tape to tie up the bunting.
 Position the next flag (in a different fabric) 6 in. (15 cm) along the tape from the first and pin it in place. Repeat for the other flags, alternating the patterns, until they are all pinned onto the tape. Machine stitch along the top edge of the flags to secure them in place.

4

Sewing basics

There are a few basics steps to follow when making things from fabric—these will help ensure that your projects turn out perfectly.

❀ Make sure the fabric you have chosen to use is suitable for the project you are intending to make. For example, pillowcases need to be made from machine-washable fabrics, while bags and throw pillowcases can be made from dry-cleanable fabrics.

❀ If possible, wash your fabric before making anything with it, so that it is preshrunk; then iron it so that all measurements and cutting are accurate.

❀ Always work on a flat, firm surface—especially when measuring and cutting fabric.

❀ If the fabric you are using frays easily, either cut it with pinking shears to create a zigzag edge that is less likely to fray, or finish the cut edge of your fabric with zigzag stitch on the sewing machine.

❀ Pin and tack fabric pieces together before sewing seams. If you are feeling lazy, you can skip the tacking, but the end results will always be better when seams are tacked first. Tacking stitches are long running stitches done by hand with a needle and thread; they are easily removed once the item has been machine stitched.

❀ If you are joining straight seams, there's no need to tack—place the pins horizontally down the seam so that the sewing machine can run smoothly over them, allowing you to leave the pins in place as you sew.

❀ After you have stitched a seam, it will need to be pressed. Do this with a hot iron (appropriate for the type of fabric you are using) and a damp tea towel. With the wrong side of the fabric facing up, open out the seam, lay the damp tea towel on top and press with an iron. This will ensure that the seam lies flat on the finished article.

No-sew ideas for small scraps

① Jam-jar covers

Cut out circles of fabric with pinking shears and use them to cover the lids of jam jars for homemade chutneys, pickles, jams, and spreads.

② Covered notebooks

Use strips of lightweight printed cotton lawn to cover a hardcover notebook, diary, or address book, creating a bound effect. You will need fabric glue and decorative paper to conceal the raw edges on the inside of the front and back covers. Overlap the edges of the fabric strips slightly, so that they become a decorative feature, and experiment with torn and pinked edges.

③ Scented sachet

For an instant scented sachet to place in your linen drawer, cut out a circle with pinking shears and place a handful of lavender in the center; gather up the fabric and twist, securing with a length of ribbon tied in a bow.

④ Felted flowers

Cut out different-sized flowers from felt, layer them up and secure with a decorative button sewn in the center. Sew onto cushions or blinds, or attach a safety pin to the back for an instant decoration for bags or clothes.

Sew it on

Ribbon in all its guises, bullion fringing, pretty buttons, tassels, glass beads, shimmering sequins, and delicate lace are must-have items for any sewing box and the icing on the cake in terms of decoration. Nothing beats a bit of luxury trimming for elevating a homespun piece into an heirloom. There is a huge array of trimmings available to buy, but keep your eyes peeled and you can amass a wonderful selection from a variety of sources. I've found handmade lace at the bottom of an auction box lot, cut buttons off coats and sequins off clothes that were being recycled, and I am always rifling through the craft store's bargain box for ribbon cast-offs.

Trimmings are an excellent way of introducing a color theme or style into a room; bedlinen trimmed with blue-and-white gingham ribbon looks fresh in a seaside home, while linen curtains edged with velvet ribbon and heavy fringing have a traditional, sophisticated feel. Combinations are endless, so don't be afraid to experiment—unexpected pairings are often the best.

Lace-trimmed towels

This is a chic way of dressing up plain towels and there are lots of possible variations—you could use ribbon instead of lace, for example. This is a good idea for family or shared bathrooms, as each person can choose their own color or pattern so there's no confusion.

Materials

Towels

Lace trim

Tape measure

Dressmaking scissors

Pins

Sewing thread

Sewing machine

1 Cut the lace to the width of the towels, adding an extra 1¼ in. (3 cm) to each length for turning the ends under.

2 Pin the lace in position, turning ⅝ in. (1.5 cm) under at each end for a neat finish. Machine stitch along both edges of the lace.

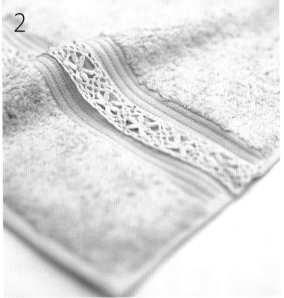

Tips

✂ Use cotton lace or ribbon that can be washed at the temperature at which you wash your towels, to avoid shrinkage and color run.

✂ If you are sewing light-colored trim onto a dark towel or vice versa, make sure that the bobbin thread in your sewing machine is the same color as your towel and the top thread is the same color as the trim.

✂ Make a hanging loop using the lace or ribbon you have used to trim the towel. To do this, cut 4¾ in. (12 cm) of lace or ribbon, turn the ends under to create neat edges, then fold the lace or ribbon in half, pin the ends together in one corner of your towel and sew in place.

Ribbon-trimmed bedlinen

Simple white bedlinen always looks great, but sometimes it's nice to add a touch of color and make it a little more personal. Here I've used gingham and initialed ribbon to freshen up a white pinstriped comforter; there are three different ways to decorate pillowcases with ribbon, too.

Materials

Double comforter

Pillowcases

2½ yards (2.2 m) of 1 in.- (25 mm-) wide blue gingham ribbon

2½ yards (2.2 m) of ⅝ in.- (15 mm-) wide yellow gingham ribbon

2½ yards (2.2 m) of ½ in.- (12 mm-) wide initialed ribbon

Tape measure

Dressmaking scissors

Pins

Tacking thread

Needle

Sewing thread

Sewing machine

Trimmed comforter

Cut the 1 in.- (25 mm-) wide blue gingham ribbon to the width of your comforter and add an extra 1¼ in. (3 cm) for turning the ends under. Pin the ribbon along the width of the comforter 6 in. (15 cm) down from the top edge. Pin the ⅝ in.- (15 mm-) wide yellow gingham ribbon 1¼ in. (3 cm) above the blue gingham ribbon. Tack both ribbons and remove the pins.

Cut the same length of initialed ribbon and position it in the center of the blue gingham ribbon. Pin and tack it in place.

Machine stitch along both edges of each ribbon to secure them; remove the tacking.

Matching trimmed pillowcase

Measure the edges of the pillowcase and add 1¼ in. (3 cm) for hems, then cut one piece of each ribbon to this length.

Pin the yellow gingham ribbon 2 in. (5 cm) in from the edge of the pillowcase and pin the blue gingham ribbon ¾ in. (2 cm) in from this, then tack both ribbons in place.

Pin and tack the initialed ribbon in the center of the blue gingham ribbon.

Machine stitch along both edges of all three ribbons; remove the tacking.

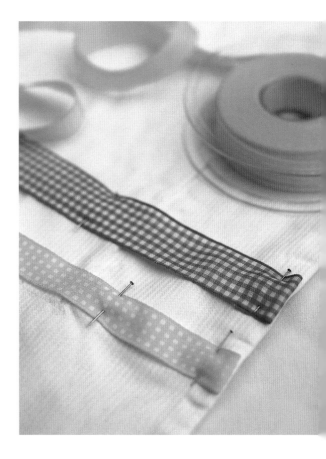

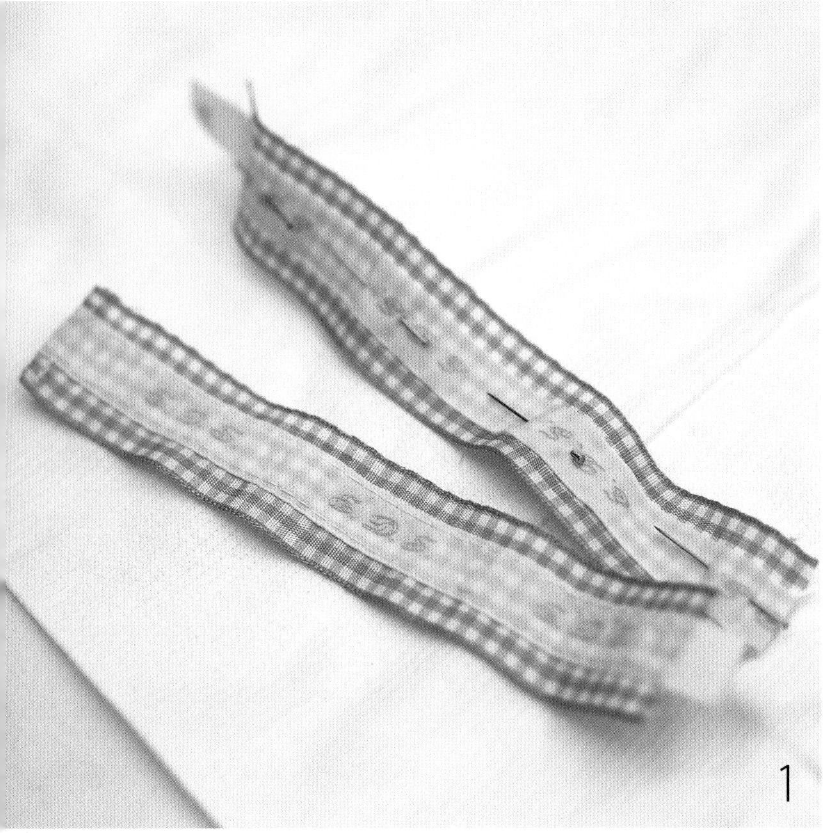

1

Bow-tied pillowcase

1 For each pillowcase with ribbon ties, cut eight 4¾ in. (12 cm) lengths of both the blue gingham ribbon and the initialed ribbon.

Position an initialed ribbon in the center of a blue gingham ribbon, then pin and tack. Machine stitch along the edges of the initialed ribbon to secure in place, then remove the tacking. Repeat to create eight ties.

2 Fold both ends of the ties under by ¼ in. (0.5 cm) and stitch down to give neat edges.

Pin one tie 4 in. (10 cm) down from the top edge of the pillowcase at the opening. Pin another tie facing it on the opposite side of the opening. Repeat for the other ties, spacing them at equal distances along both sides of the opening (four ties on each side).

Machine stitch, then tie the four pairs of ribbons in bows to close the pillowcase.

2

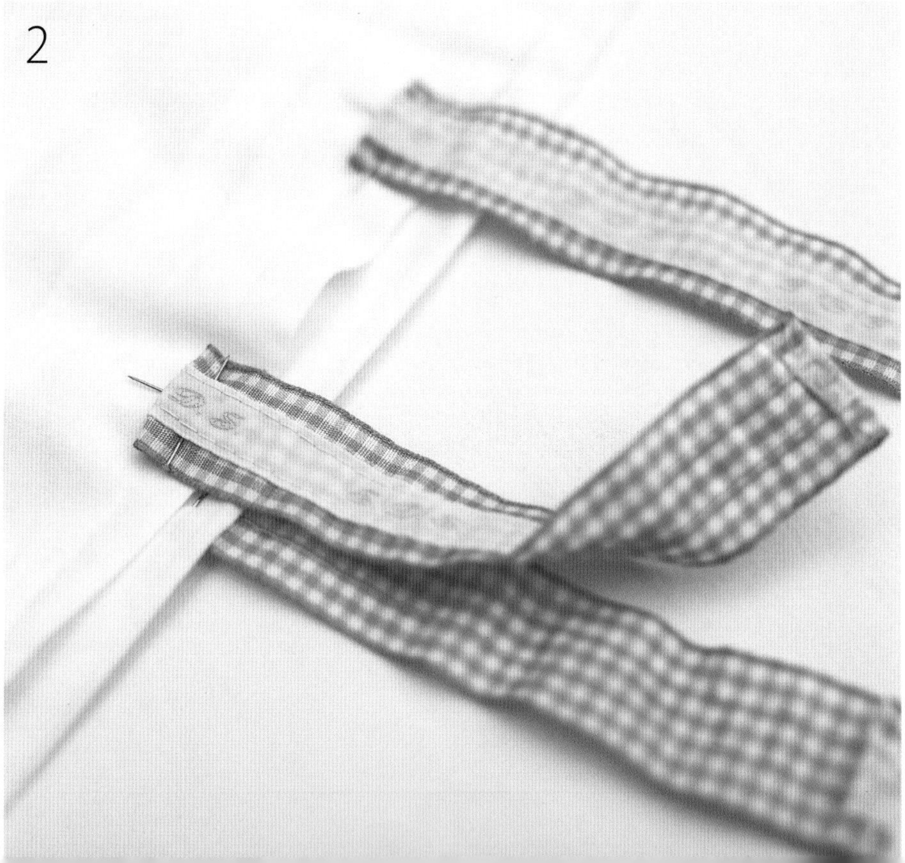

Tips

- Choose ribbons that can be machine washed and are color safe.
- Sew as close to the edge of the ribbon as possible to give a neat finish and to prevent the edges from curling over.

Oxford pillowcase

Measure the length and width of the border of an Oxford pillowcase, add them together and double the total, then add 1¼ in. (3 cm) for turning the ends under. Cut a piece of initialed ribbon to this length.

Pin the ribbon onto the pillowcase border, easing it neatly around the corners. Tack, then machine stitch and remove the tacking.

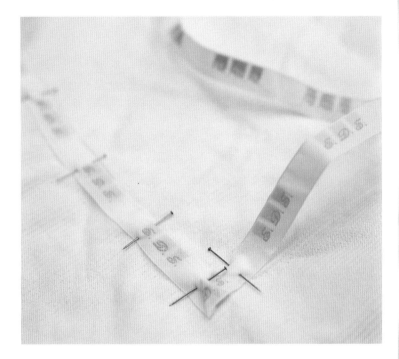

More ideas

✂ Coordinate your curtains with your ribbon-trimmed bedlinen by stitching a length of the same ribbon down the inner long edge of each curtain panel, so that they hang side by side when drawn closed. Set the ribbon a good distance in from the edge of the curtain so that it can be clearly seen when they are drawn.

✂ Cut down old sheets and trim them with pictorial ribbon for a child's cot or bed. Hardwearing jacquard ribbons are a good choice, as they can withstand heavy laundering.

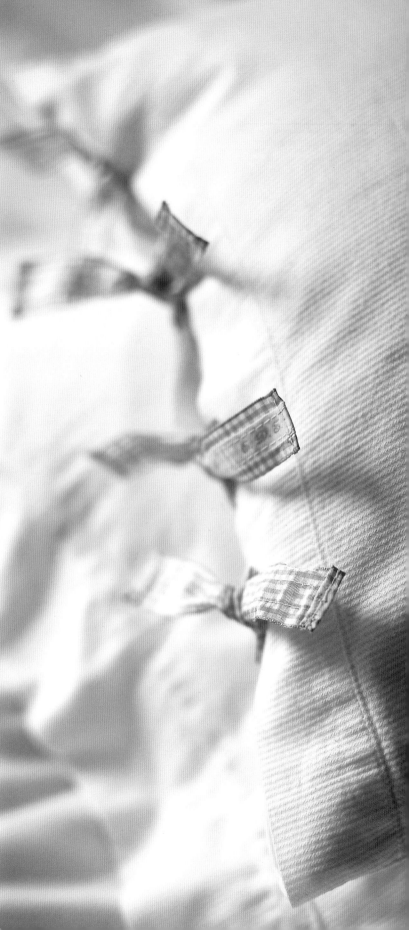

Button-and-shell-decorated curtain panel

This is a simple if slightly time-consuming way to decorate a curtain panel, but if you spend a few hours sewing in front of the TV, you'll have it finished in no time. I used two rows of buttons interspersed with a row of shells, but three rows of buttons will look just as effective.

Materials

Curtain panel

Selection of buttons and shells (with predrilled holes)

Ruler

Fabric pen

Tape measure

Needle

Sewing thread

Scissors

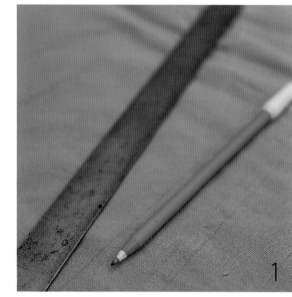

1 Using a ruler and fabric pen, start by drawing a line along the vertical drop of the curtain, 2 in. (5 cm) in from the edge.

Draw another parallel vertical line 1¾ in. (4 cm) in from the first line and then a third line 1¾ in. (4 cm) from the second line.

2 Working on a large flat surface, arrange buttons and shells as you wish along the first line, making sure that they look balanced and are evenly spaced.

Starting at the top and working down, sew the buttons and shells to the curtain using thread the same color as your curtain for a uniform look.

Repeat for the subsequent two rows.

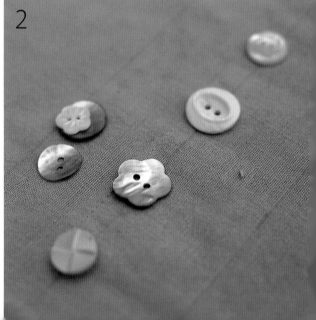

Tips

- Although I used neutral-colored curtains with toning buttons and shells, this project would work just as well using richly colored fabric.

- For a bold and upbeat look, use multicolored buttons and attach them with contrasting brightly colored threads.

- Rows of buttons could also be worked all the way across a curtain panel or blind. If you decide to do this, for your sanity, stick to small window coverings or you'll still be sewing this project in your old age.

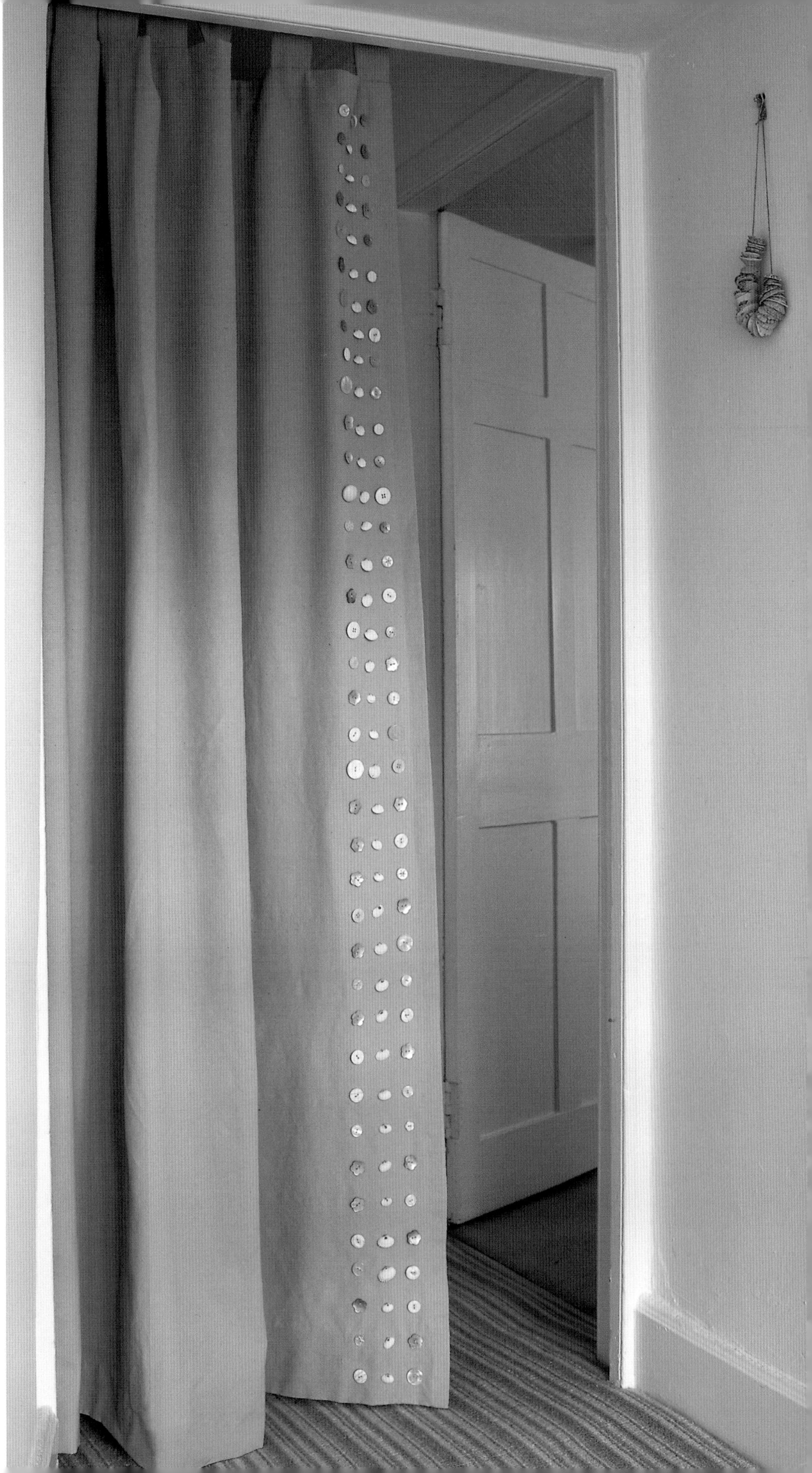

Ribbon-and-fabric-flower cushion

This pretty cushion uses two different methods for making flowers from scraps of ribbon, trim and fabric. The flowers are then stitched onto the cushion cover and embellished with beads. Try using ribbons and trims in various widths, so that the flowers you make are different sizes—this will help make the design look balanced. For the flowers made from scraps of fabric, light- to medium-weight fabrics work best.

CUT 2

Materials

Cushion cover and pad

63 in. (160 cm) of 1½ in-(36 mm-) wide satin ribbon

24 in. (60 cm) of 1½ in-(36 mm-) wide sequinned or lace trim

Scraps of fabric

Flower templates

Fourteen ⅛ in. (3 mm) beads

Tape measure

Dressmaking scissors

Needle

Sewing thread

Fabric pen

Pins

8 x 4 in. (20 x 10 cm) of nonfraying fabric, such as felt

Fabric glue

CUT 4

TRACE OFF THE TEMPLATES, SHOWN HERE AT ACTUAL SIZE

Ribbon flower

1 Cut a piece of satin ribbon 8 in. (20 cm) long. Thread a needle with two strands of matching thread and sew running stitch (see pages 88–9) along one edge of the length of ribbon.

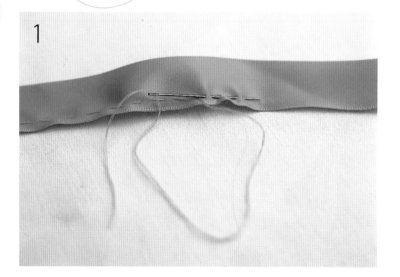

2 Tightly gather the ribbon on the thread to create a flower and secure with a knot, leaving a long tail of thread so that you can attach a bead later. If the ribbon ends look untidy, sew them together so that the raw edges face toward the back of the flower.

4

2

3 Thread a bead onto the long tail of thread that you left in step 2. Hold the bead in position in the center of the flower and secure it with a couple of stitches on the back of the flower.

Make seven more ribbon flowers in this way. Then, using the same technique, make three flowers using sequinned or lace trim instead of ribbon.

Fabric flower

4 Using a fabric pen and the templates on page 56, cut out two large petal shapes and four small petal shapes for each flower. You can use all the same fabric or mix and match. Cut into the fabric along the dotted lines indicated on the templates.

5

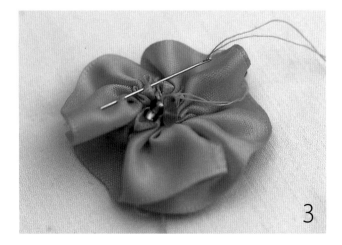

3

5 Lay the two large petal shapes on top of one another, with the fabric right sides up. Fold the four smaller petals in half. Lay one on top of the large petals, then lay the next folded petal on top of this, so that it overlaps a quarter of the first folded petal.

6 Add the next folded petal so that it overlaps a quarter of the previous petal. Repeat for the last folded petal, so that they are all overlapping, and hold in place with a pin.

7 Using a needle and thread, secure all the petals with a few stitches in the center of the flower. Slip a bead over the needle, hold it in the center of the flower and secure on the back with a few stitches.
Make two more flowers in the same way.

Assembling the decorations

8 Cut a small disc of nonfraying fabric and glue it to the rear of each flower you have made.
Arrange the flowers on the cushion cover and pin them in place. Using a needle and thread, stitch the fabric-disc backing on each flower to the cushion cover.

Tip

 Add more decoration to the cushion cover by randomly scattering sequins around the ribbon and fabric flowers. Attach using two stitches on either side of each sequin to hold it in place. (Using two stitches rather than one will prevent the sequins from moving around.)

Camping blanket

I unearthed this old army blanket, belonging to Great-Uncle Jack, while clearing out my parents's attic, and the badges that I had amassed as a kid had been kicking around in my sewing box for years. It seemed a good idea to put the two together and use the blanket for camping trips or just for lolling around on outdoors.

Materials

Thick blanket

Selection of badges

Pins

Needle

Sewing thread

Scissors

Tips

✂ When arranging badges, work from the center outward. Basing the design on a geometric shape, such as a square, rectangle, cross, or diamond (as here), will help keep it looking balanced.

✂ You can group badges by type, color, or shape—whatever works best for you.

1 Lay the blanket flat on the floor and arrange the badges on it. Arrange the badges by eye—there's no need to use a tape measure to work out the spacing between them. When you are happy with the design, pin the badges in position.

2 Using thread the same color as your blanket, hand-sew the badges to the blanket with slip stitch. Secure the end of the thread with a couple of stitches positioned so that they will be hidden by the badge. Next, pick up a couple of threads in your blanket and then slide the needle through the edge of the badge, picking up just a couple of threads, and pull the needle through. Repeat all around the badge.

Ribbons and trimmings

Adding decorative trimming to a finished project is often all that is needed to transform it from ordinary into something special. No piece of trimming is too small to be of use—odds and ends of lace and ribbon stitched side by side onto a cushion cover have a boho feel, while fringing glued around a lampshade will give it a more luxurious look.

There are a multitude of trimmings to suit all tastes and needs, so whether you are a maximalist into masses of color and decoration or prefer things pared down and simple, there's a trimming for you. Think beyond ribbons and tassels and look for more unusual items, such as crystal fringing that could be used to edge a pelmet, or fancy feathers that could add a decorative dimension to a floral corsage. Alternatively, use buttons to add pattern and detail to plain fabrics or stitch rows of opalescent buttons onto a cushion cover in simple geometric patterns.

Beads are great for adding a bit of glamour; tiny glass beads will give a delicate shimmer to embroidery, while chunkier bugle beads can be used to add weight and a jewel-like finish to brocade or velvet. And don't dismiss a length of utilitarian cotton webbing—it is perfect for binding floor coverings, or for making ties for aprons or handles for a tote bag.

Types of ribbon

① Sheer

This group covers any ribbon made from fine gauzy material such as georgette and organdy. This type of ribbon is good for making big floppy bows or ruffles, as the loose weave means that it is less structured than satin ribbon.

② Satin and taffeta

These are among the most popular types of ribbon and come in a multitude of colors and patterns. They can be single- or double-faced: the single-faced version is shiny on one side and matte on the other, while double-faced satin ribbons are shiny on both sides. Satin and taffeta ribbons aren't necessarily made of silk; more often they are made of polyester, which is cheaper to buy.

③ Jacquard

This is a woven ribbon incorporating a pattern that is textured like damask woven fabric. Jacquard ribbon is usually hardwearing and is a good choice for decorating items that need to be washed regularly (always check a ribbon's washing instructions).

④ Grosgrain

A ribbed ribbon that is quite thick, grosgrain was traditionally used for millinery. Available in lots of colors and often striped, it has a neat, structured look.

---

10 IDEAS for using ribbon

1   Use lengths of ribbon to disguise or embellish patchwork seams on cushions and throws.

2   Extra-wide ribbon can be used to bind the edges of blankets and sheets. Choose tactile materials, such as satin and velvet, which will feel good against your skin.

3   String chunky beads onto a narrow ribbon to make a necklace, keeping the beads in place with a knot after the last bead at each end of the ribbon, or knotting between each bead.

4   Glue lengths of colored rickrack or gingham ribbon onto a lampshade in a child's bedroom. Choose bright, fresh colors that will help to inject a sense of fun.

5   Use a length of grosgrain ribbon to hang a mirror or picture and tie a bow at the top to hide the hanging hook.

6   Combine wide velvet ribbon and silk satin ribbon to make decadent curtain tiebacks. Don't stint on the ribbon—wrap it several times around the curtain, then tie it in a simple knot and leave the ends to tumble down the curtain.

7   Edge a tablecloth and placemats with ribbon. Choose two or three ribbons in different colors and widths and simply stitch them on inset from the edge of the cloth.

8   As an alternative to giftwrap, wrap bottles of wine, olive oil, or bath oil in fabric and finish off with a length of wide ribbon tied in a bow.

9   Organza ribbon tied in a big bow makes an impromptu napkin ring; tuck a flower into the knot for a more romantic look. For special occasions, use a length of ribbon to tie a flower or bunch of berries to the back of dining chairs.

10   Trim the lids of storage boxes with grosgrain ribbon held in place with fabric glue.

Cover it up

Appliqué is the perfect medium for using up odds and ends of fabric. Any fabric can be used as long as it can be sewn, so experiment with organza, muslin, net, velvet, crepe de chine, georgette, satin, wool, cord, felt, leather, suede, and even plastic-coated fabrics such as vinyl. As well as being a method for covering up tears or stains, appliqué is a fairly easy way of applying decoration to a fabric that can then be further embellished with beading or embroidery. Almost anything goes in terms of mixing different types of fabric—as seen in the project on page 70, where juxtaposing satin with brushed cotton transforms a plain cushion cover into an item of luxury. There are several ways of attaching appliqué shapes to fabric. Running stitch and backstitch, whether sewn on the machine or by hand, are the fastest and add emphasis to the outlines of shapes. Decorative chain stitch is especially good for securing curved shapes. Buttonhole stitch works well on fabrics that fray easily. (For instructions for these stitches, see pages 88–9.)

Flower-power lampshade

Give a lampshade a retro feel with this bold floral decoration that is fast to do and requires no sewing. Choose strong colors and graphic patterns and, if you wish, glue a coordinating band of ribbon around the top and bottom edges of the shade.

Materials

Lampshade—the one shown here has a circumference of 34 in. (86 cm)

Scraps of fabric in 3 or 4 different colors and/or patterns

Iron-on interfacing

Iron and ironing board

Flower templates

Fabric pen

Dressmaking scissors

Double-sided tape

Fabric glue

TRACE OFF THE TEMPLATES, SHOWN HERE AT ACTUAL SIZE

Tip

✄ Choose fabrics that don't fray easily so that the edges don't require stitching.

1 Attach iron-on interfacing to the back of your fabric scraps, following the manufacturer's instructions. (The interfacing will help prevent the fabric from fraying.)

Position the templates on the interfacing and trace around them with a fabric pen. Carefully cut out enough floral motifs to decorate your lampshade. (For a lampshade with a circumference of 34 in. (86 cm), I used three of each large template in four different fabrics and the same for the smaller template.)

2

2 Cut small strips of double-sided tape and stick them to the back of the motifs, then arrange the motifs on the lampshade. Here the motifs have been randomly scattered over the shade, but you can arrange them in ordered rows if you prefer.

Once you are happy with the position of the motifs, remove one, peel off the double-sided tape and apply glue to the back of the motif. Be careful not to use too much glue, as this can leave marks on the fabric that will be visible. Stick the motif onto the lampshade, pressing around all the edges to make sure that they are stuck down. Repeat for the remaining motifs.

Floral appliqué cushion

Appliqué is a relatively fast method of creating pattern and texture. Designs can be loose and made up of floral motifs or scrolling shapes, or they can be more uniform. Stars and hearts laid out in a simple grid formation on a white linen background have a homespun appeal and would make a great quilt for a cot or child's bed.

Materials

Cushion cover

Remnant of patterned dress fabric

Iron-on fabric adhesive

Iron and ironing board

Dressmaking scissors

Pins

Needle

Tacking thread

Sewing thread

Sewing machine

Dressmaker's chalk or fabric pen

Embroidery thread

1 Iron the sheet of fabric adhesive to the back of your chosen fabric, following the manufacturer's instructions.

Using a sharp pair of dressmaking scissors, cut out a selection of appliqué motifs from the patterned fabric.

2 Arrange the appliqué motifs on the cushion cover. When you are happy with the design, pin them in place.

3 Using a needle and tacking thread, tack the motifs to the cushion cover using two or three stitches per motif.

Following the manufacturer's instructions, apply the iron to fuse the appliqué motifs onto the cushion cover. Remove the tacking.

4 Set the sewing machine to zigzag stitch, using a small- to medium-width stitch that is close together (almost buttonhole is ideal), and sew around the edges of each motif. Work slowly, in good light, making sure that you cover all the raw edges. When you need to change direction, lift the foot of the sewing machine, leaving the needle in the fabric.

Add extra decoration and link the motifs together with running stitch, using a needle and three strands of embroidery thread. If you are nervous about stitching freehand, draw a line first with dressmaker's chalk or a fabric pen and follow that as you sew.

Tips

✂ Experiment with different types of materials but avoid using fabrics that stretch (such as jersey) or fray easily, as they are tricky to work with. Fabrics prone to fraying should be backed with dressmaker's iron-on backing or interfacing.

✂ To prevent the fabric from puckering when you are sewing by hand or on the machine, use a frame or embroidery hoop to stretch the fabric and keep it taut.

Tea party tablecloth

Tablecloths are fast becoming a thing of the past, but they are perfect for dressing up an old table and adding a touch of refinement to a cup of tea and a slice of cake with friends. This project uses simple embroidery stitches: buttonhole and backstitch. If you haven't done them before, practice first on a scrap of fabric. Aim for neat, even stitches and don't be afraid to unpick any you're not happy with—if you don't, they'll be the only thing you notice every time you use the tablecloth.

Materials

Square or rectangular tablecloth

Scraps of fabric for floral motifs

Flower and leaf templates

Tracing paper

Pencil or ballpoint pen

Dressmaker's carbon paper

Dressmaking scissors

Pins

Needle

Tacking thread

Embroidery hoop

Embroidery thread

TRACE OFF THE TEMPLATES, SHOWN HERE AT ACTUAL SIZE

1 Trace each motif and embroidery pattern onto tracing paper. To transfer these onto your fabric, place a sheet of dressmaker's carbon paper colored side down on top of your fabric. Place the tracing motifs on top of this and secure in place with a few pins. Using a pencil or ballpoint pen, trace around the design. This will leave a light chalk pattern on the fabric for you to follow, which can be easily brushed off when you have finished sewing. Dressmaker's carbon paper comes in lots of different colors—choose a color that contrasts with your fabric so that it is easily visible.

2 Cut out 12 of each motif and arrange them on each corner and along the edge of your tablecloth as shown in the picture on page 75. Pin and then tack the motifs in place.

3 Secure the section of fabric you are going to embroider in an embroidery hoop. This holds the fabric taut so that it is easier to work with and prevents puckering. Using a needle threaded with four strands of embroidery thread, sew around the edges of each motif in buttonhole stitch (see pages 88–9) to secure it in place. Repeat this process, stitching around all the edges of the flower and leaf motifs. Remove the tacking.

4 Using six strands of embroidery thread and backstitch (see pages 88–9), fill in the leaf veins and patterning in the flower centers and finish with a French knot (see step 5 on page 85).

3

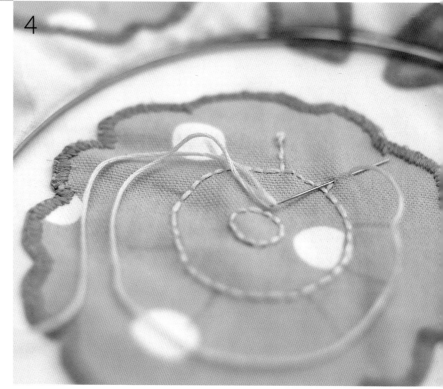

4

Tip

✂ If you are pressed for time or don't enjoy embroidering by hand, you can stitch this project on the sewing machine, but it won't have quite the same handmade charm. If you choose to use the machine, use a wide zigzag stitch with little space in between the stitches to attach the flower motifs, and use running stitch to fill in the detail in the center of the flowers.

Large-scale appliqué chair cover

Transform an armchair into a statement-making piece of furniture by decorating it with giant appliqué. The technique is the same as for the floral appliqué cushion on page 70, just scaled up, so there's no need to be nervous. I applied appliqué motifs to a loose cover, but you can also apply them to a chair with fixed upholstery—it just means that the appliqué will need to be stitched on by hand, using a curved upholstery needle rather than on the sewing machine.

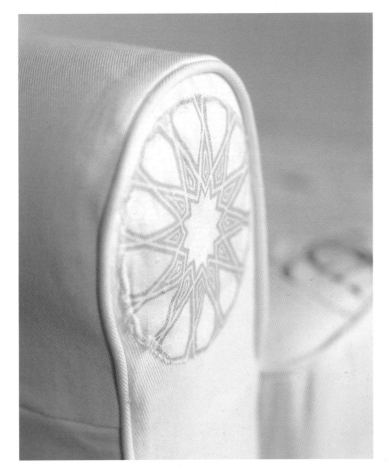

Materials

Chair with loose cover

Fabric with a large-scale floral or foliate pattern

Iron-on adhesive

Iron and ironing board

Dressmaking scissors

Pins

Needle

Tacking thread

Sewing thread

Sewing machine

1 Start by attaching the iron-on adhesive to the back of your patterned fabric, following the manufacturer's instructions.

Cut out a selection of floral and foliate motifs from your patterned fabric. Think about the shape of your chair and how you would like to decorate it: a large branching stem across the back of the chair, for example, will have visual impact and provide a structure around which you can arrange your other motifs.

Tip

✂ You can embellish the appliqué with embroidery, but restrict this to areas that receive less wear, such as the sides of the chair.

1

2 Pin the motifs onto your chair, playing around with the positioning until you are happy with the overall design. Try to connect different parts of the chair by trailing part of a motif across different sections of the chair. Overlap the motifs, as well, and don't be afraid to leave space between them.

2

3

3 Tack the motifs to the chair cover and remove the pins. Then, if you are working on a loose cover, take it off the chair. Iron the appliqué motifs to fuse them to the cover, following the manufacturer's instructions. (If you are working on fixed upholstery, carefully apply the iron to the patches directly on the chair.)

Stitch the edges of the motifs with zigzag stitch on your machine (or by hand with a curved upholstery needle). Remove the tacking. Iron or steam away any creases, then replace the cover on the chair.

Decorated apron

There are two ways of tackling this project—you can either make the apron from scratch using the template below, or simply decorate a ready-made apron. If you are doing the latter, it is very simple to add a pocket by following the instructions from step 3. Choosing a contrasting fabric for the pocket will help the appliqué decoration to stand out.

Materials

Apron and cupcake templates

1 yard (1 m) of fabric for apron

2 yards (2 m) of 1 in.- (25 mm-) wide tape for apron ties

14 x 9 in. (36 x 23 cm) of contrasting fabric for pocket

10½ x 7 in. (27 x 17 cm) of fabric for patch

Scraps of fabric for cupcakes

Dressmaking scissors

Pins

Sewing thread

Sewing machine

Iron and ironing board

Tape measure

Embroidery thread and needle

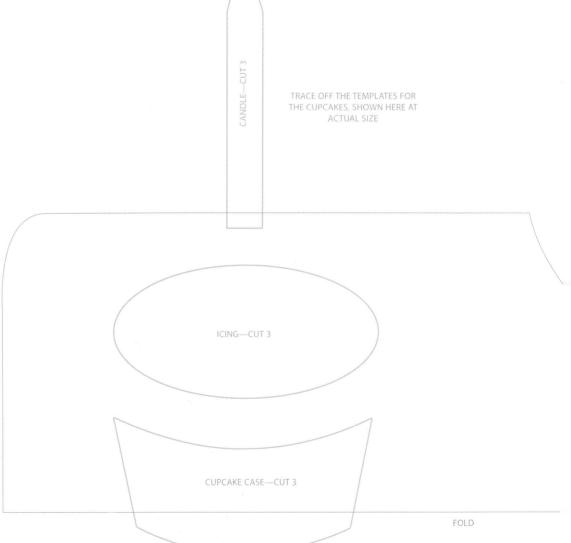

CANDLE—CUT 3

TRACE OFF THE TEMPLATES FOR THE CUPCAKES, SHOWN HERE AT ACTUAL SIZE

ICING—CUT 3

CUPCAKE CASE—CUT 3

FOLD

1 To make the apron, enlarge the template below by 400 percent, then fold the fabric in half and cut out the apron shape.

Finish the edges by folding the raw edges under by ¼ in. (0.5 cm) and then under again by another ¼ in. (0.5 cm) and pin. Machine stitch, then press the edges flat.

USE THIS APRON TEMPLATE
ENLARGED AT 400 PERCENT
IF YOU ARE MAKING YOUR
OWN APRON

3 Cut out the pocket and patch. Then, using the templates on page 82, cut out three candles and three cupcakes. Arrange the cakes in a line centrally on the patch and pin them in place, then pin the candles on the cakes.

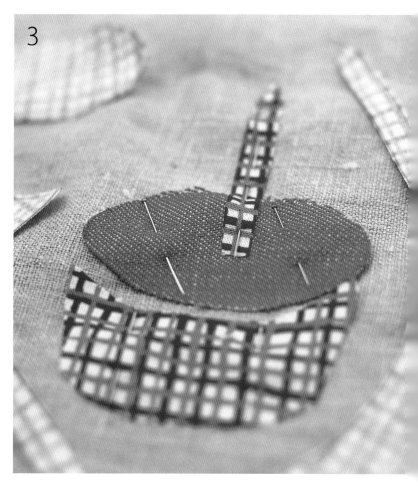

2 Attach the apron ties. For the neck loop, cut a piece of tape measuring 24½ in. (62 cm) and turn the raw edges under at both ends. Pin one end on the back of the apron at each side of the top edge.

For the waist ties, cut two pieces of tape measuring approximately 24 in. (60 cm) and turn the raw edges under at both ends. Pin one end of each tape on the back of the apron at the waist, making sure that the ties are at the same height on both sides. Machine stitch the ties in place.

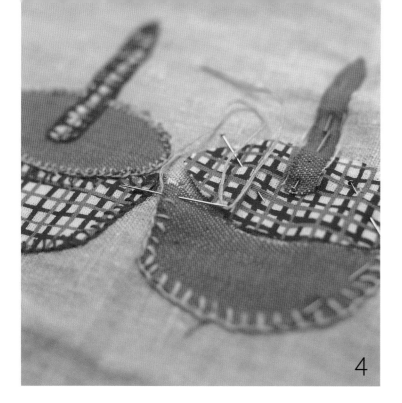

4

4 Using a needle and three strands of embroidery thread, sew along all the edges of the cakes and candles with blanket stitch (see pages 88–9) to attach them to the patch.

5 Decorate the icing on the outer two cakes with French knots, using a needle and three strands of embroidery thread. Bring the needle up from the back through to the front of the fabric and coil the thread around the needle two or three times. Insert the needle back into the fabric as close to where it came through as possible and pull to tighten the thread into a knot.

To make a flame at the top of each candle, sew three long vertical stitches side by side using a needle and three strands of embroidery thread.

5

6

6 Turn the top edge of the pocket under by ¼ in. (0.5 cm) and then again by another ¼ in. (0.5 cm). Pin and machine stitch.

Turn the edges of the patch under by ¼ in. (0.5 cm) and pin. Position the patch in the center of the pocket, pin it in place, and machine stitch around all four edges.

Position the pocket on the apron so that the top edge is approximately at waist height. Turn the side and bottom edges under by ¼ in. (0.5 cm), pin and machine stitch, then press.

Fabric adornment

Decorative appliqué motifs can be attached to a base fabric with a variety of hand-embroidery stitches. You can also embroider extra detail on the motifs before cutting them out and applying them to the ground fabric, using an embroidery hoop to keep the fabric taut. Overleaf are four of the simplest stitches to get you started—running stitch, backstitch, chain stitch, and buttonhole/blanket stitch.

In addition, you can glue sequins or sew beads onto appliqué motifs for a touch of shimmer, but remember that you will need to dry clean or very gently hand-wash the fabric, so use this form of decoration only on items that won't need regular laundering. Appliqué offers many other creative possibilities for decoration. Below are some ideas.

Pebble pattern

Combine appliqué with embroidery by cutting out simple pebble shapes from plain-colored fabrics, scatter them over a cushion cover and use running stitch to attach them. Next, using backstitch and embroidery thread that matches the appliqué motifs, sew more pebble shapes on the cushion to create a modern abstract pattern. Make sure that the design is balanced by having more stitched pebble motifs than appliqué ones.

Photo appliqué

Use heat-transfer paper to apply a favorite family photo, pet portrait, or landscape onto a remnant of fabric to create a pictorial appliqué. A great idea for personalized presents, the transferred motif can be added to bags, cushion covers, or even pillowcases and combined with related appliqué motifs in plain or patterned fabrics to build up a design.

Wall hanging

If you are feeling adventurous, use appliqué techniques to create a wall hanging depicting a story. For a child's room, you could illustrate a nursery rhyme or produce a prehistoric landscape populated with dinosaurs. Make your own patterns by tracing simplified images from books and cut them out in fabric—the only limiting factor is your imagination.

❶ Running stitch

This is the easiest of straight stitches and involves simply taking the needle in and out of the fabric in a line. Try to get a rhythm going, as it will help keep the stitches even with regular spaces in between. Use running stitch to outline a motif. Working from right to left if you are right-handed or left to right if you are left-handed, bring the needle up from the back of the fabric through to the front and take several small stitches on the point of the needle before pulling the thread through. If the fabric you are working with is particularly thick, you may need to make each stitch individually.

❷ Backstitch

This is very similar to running stitch but is made with no gaps between stitches to create a continual line. Working from right to left if you are right-handed or left to right if you are left-handed, bring the needle up from the back of the fabric through to the front and make a small stitch backward, reinserting the needle an equal stitch length in front of where you started.

❸ Chain stitch

Chain stitch can be worked from top to bottom (as shown) or right to left if you are right-handed or left to right if you are

left-handed; just turn the fabric as needed. Bring the needle up from the back of the fabric through to the front and make a small stitch forward but do not pull the thread through. Loop the working thread under the tip of the needle as shown then pull the needle through, making one chain link. Reinsert the needle through the same hole the thread emerged from, make another stitch, loop the thread under the needle tip as before, and pull the thread through, making another link.

❹ Buttonhole/blanket stitch

Buttonhole and blanket stitch are worked in the same way, but for buttonhole stitch the stitches are placed close together with no gap between them to make a solid line of stitches, whereas a gap is left between stitches for blanket stitch (shown). Work from right to left if you are right-handed or left to right if you are left-handed. Bring the needle up from the back of the fabric through to the front so that it emerges on the outer edge of the motif. Make a vertical stitch, about 1/8–1/4 in. (3–5 mm) long, push the needle back through the fabric and then bring it back through to the front again next to where you started. Loop the thread under the needle and pull through to create a stitch.

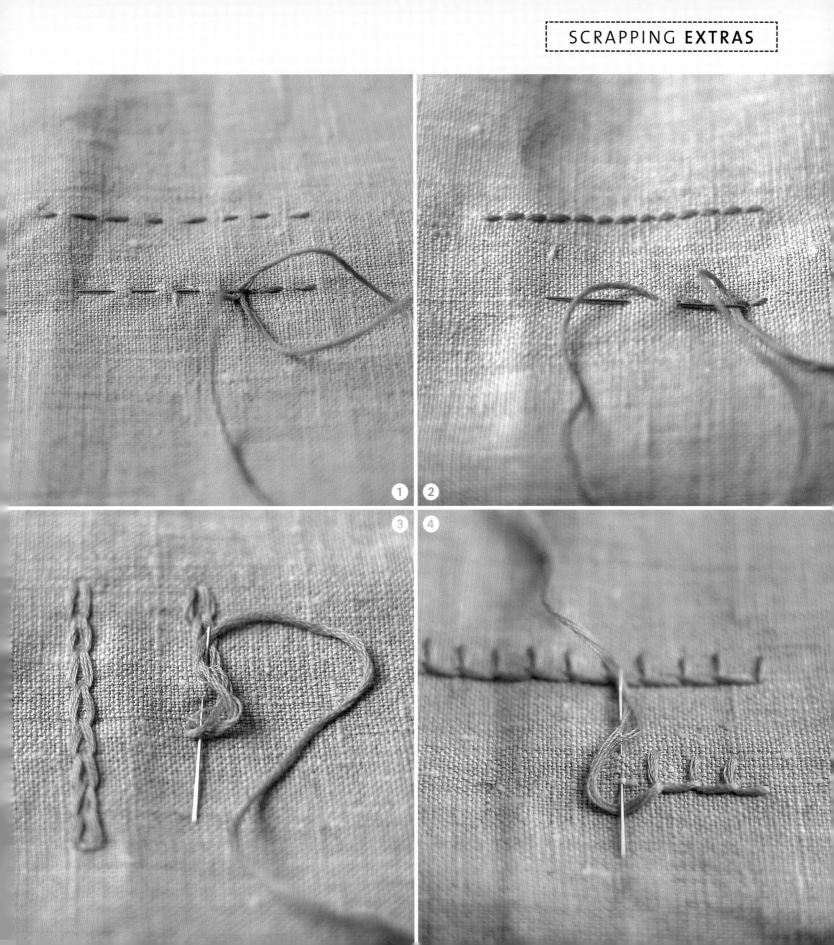

Mix it up

Patchwork is the perfect technique for habitual hoarders of fabric scraps and, as it requires tiny pieces, it truly is a thrift craft. The designs we're familiar with evolved in the eighteenth century, when small pieces of cloth were stitched together to make bedspreads and were often quilted for extra warmth. Simple geometric shapes—squares, rectangles, triangles, and diamonds—were combined to make graphic patterns. Templates were developed to speed up the process and ensure a uniform pattern.

Use of color and planning is key to a successful patchwork. Contrasting tones and mixing plain and patterned fabrics will add pace and help make a design dynamic. When creating a single-color patchwork, include a balance of pale-, mid-, and dark-toned fabrics, and add a touch of white for contrast. When cutting out patches from a patterned fabric, think about positioning. If you are using a floral fabric, for example, placing the flower in the center of the patch will help the finished patchwork look balanced.

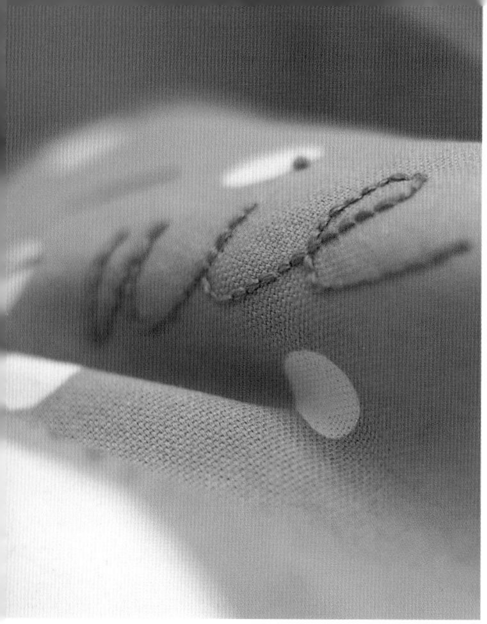

Personalized patched cushion

This quick-to-make personalized cushion takes a modern and loose approach to patchwork and makes a unique present for a newborn baby, teenage girl, close friend, or even your grandma. The one here is decorated with cut-out flowers and a bird motif, but you could use other images, such as a dog in the central patch with stars or hearts scattered across the rest of the cushion.

Materials

- 15 x 15 in. (38 x 38 cm) cushion pad
- 12½ x 12½ in. (32 x 32 cm) of polka-dot fabric
- 2 strips of striped fabric 4¾ x 16 in. (12 x 41 cm) and 4¾ x 12½ in. (12 x 32 cm)
- 2 pieces of fabric 10½ x 16 in. (27 x 41 cm) for the back of the cushion
- 5 x 5 in. (13 x 13 cm) of white fabric for the patch
- Scraps of floral fabric for cut-out flowers and bird motif
- Dressmaking scissors
- Tape measure
- Iron-on interfacing
- Iron and ironing board
- Bird template
- Pins
- Needle
- Tacking thread
- Sewing thread
- Sewing machine
- Fabric pen
- Ruler
- Embroidery thread and hoop

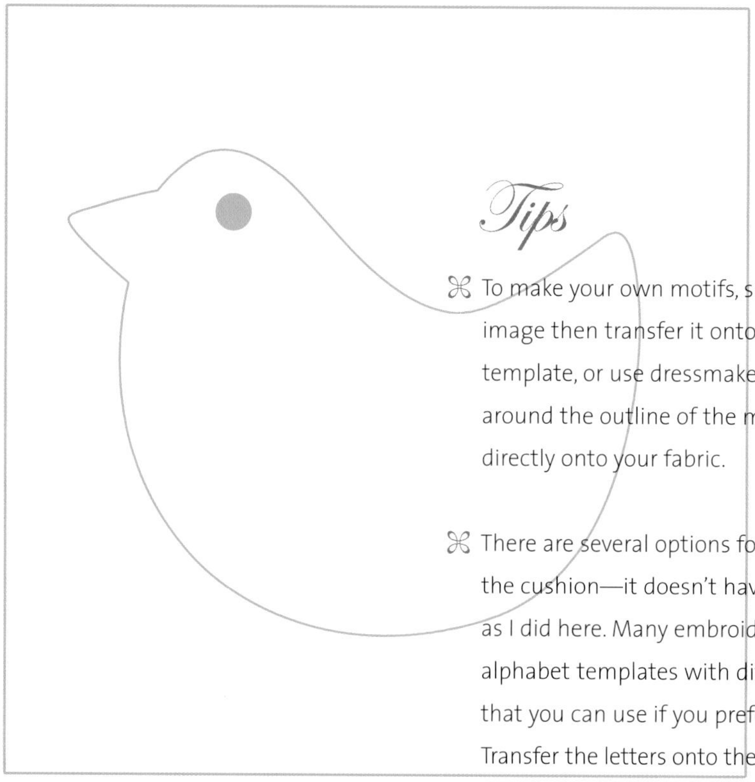

TRACE OFF THE BIRD TEMPLATE, SHOWN HERE AT ACTUAL SIZE. THE PATCH SHOWN IS THE SIZE OF THE HEMMED PATCH, SO ADD AN EXTRA 5/8 in. (1.5 cm) ALL AROUND

Tips

- To make your own motifs, simply trace your chosen image then transfer it onto cardboard and cut out a template, or use dressmaker's carbon paper and trace around the outline of the motif to transfer the image directly onto your fabric.
- There are several options for stitching the name onto the cushion—it doesn't have to be written freehand, as I did here. Many embroidery pattern books contain alphabet templates with different styles of script that you can use if you prefer a more uniform look. Transfer the letters onto the cushion using dressmaker's carbon paper and fill them in with long vertical stitches placed close together side by side (satin stitch).
- When choosing fabrics, lay them next to each other roughly folded into the three patches that make up the cushion, so you can make sure that they work together.

1 Cut out all the fabric pieces required for the front and back of the cushion cover.

Attach iron-on interfacing to the back of the floral fabric, applying an iron according to the manufacturer's instructions.

Cut out three flowers (choosing different shapes and sizes to give a bit of variety), then trace around the bird template and cut this out as well.

3 Pin the bird-motif patch centrally on the polka-dot fabric, 2 in. (5 cm) up from the bottom edge. Arrange the fabric flowers to the top right of the patch and pin them in place. When you are happy with the arrangement, tack the flowers and patch to the polka-dot fabric, then machine stitch them in place and remove the tacking.

2 Take the small white patch of fabric measuring 5 x 5 in. (13 x 13 cm) and turn the edges under by ⅝ in. (1.5 cm). Pin and then tack.

Position the bird motif in the center of the patch and tack it in place. Then machine stitch around the edge of the motif. Remove the tacking and press.

4 Using a fabric pen, write a name in the space in the top left of the polka-dot patch and draw a circle for the bird's eye. Then, using a ruler, draw three lines on both sides of the bird-motif patch at ½ in. (1 cm) intervals. Mark two lines in the same way ½ in. (1 cm) from the top of the patch, extending them to meet the top of the lines you have drawn at the sides (see photograph on page 93).

Using three strands of embroidery thread, fill in the eye by laying stitches down next to each other until the circle is filled. Use an embroidery hoop to keep the fabric taut. Using six strands of embroidery thread, stitch the name in backstitch (see pages 88–9). Also with six strands of thread, stitch along the lines in running stitch (see pages 88–9).

5 With right sides together and a ⅝ in. (1.5 cm) seam, pin then machine stitch the 4¾ x 12½ in. (12 x 32 cm) strip to the left edge of the polka-dot square. Press the seams open. Then attach the bottom 4¾ x 16 in. (12 x 41 cm) strip.

6 Turn one long edge of both back cover pieces over on itself twice to conceal the raw edges. Pin and machine stitch.

Place the two back pieces of the cushion cover on top of the front piece, with right sides together. The hemmed edges of the back pieces should overlap each other by 2 in. (5 cm).

Allowing a ⅝ in. (1.5 cm) seam, pin, tack, then machine stitch all around the edges of the cover. Remove the tacking, trim the corners and press the seams open. Turn the cover right sides out and insert the cushion pad.

Patchwork tea cozy and coffeepot sleeve

These jolly tea- and coffeepot cozies are made by piecing together strips of material to create a fabric from which you can then make your cozy—it's patchwork at its fastest and simplest. You can add detail with a machine-stitched and appliquéd cup-and-saucer panel. If you are short of time and energy, you could skip this last step and use boldly patterned fabrics for maximum impact instead.

Materials

For the tea cozy:

Tea cozy, cup, and saucer templates

12 strips of fabric 11 x 3½ in. (28 x 9 cm) for the outer cover

2 pieces of fabric 15 x 10¼ in. (38 x 26 cm) for the lining

2 pieces of lightweight batting 15 x 10¼ in. (38 x 26 cm)

4 x 4 in. (10 x 10 cm) linen patch

Scrap of fabric for the cup

Pins

Sewing thread

Sewing machine

Iron and ironing board

Fabric pen

Pinking shears

Needle

Fabric glue

Embroidery thread

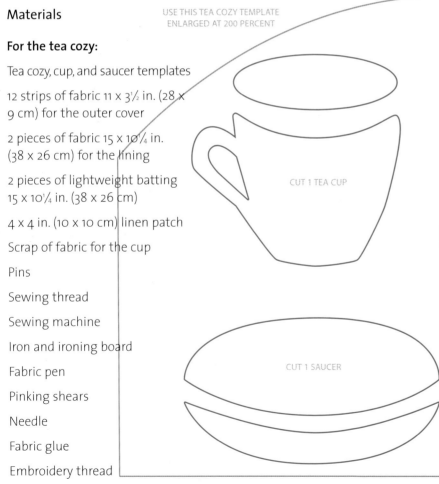

USE THIS TEA COZY TEMPLATE
ENLARGED AT 200 PERCENT

CUT 1 TEA CUP

FOLD

CUT 1 SAUCER

TRACE OFF THE TEMPLATES FOR THE CUP
AND SAUCER, SHOWN HERE AT ACTUAL SIZE

Tea cozy

1 Start by joining the strips of fabric to make two patched pieces for the cozy's outer cover. With right sides facing and a ½ in. (1 cm) seam, pin two strips together along their length, then machine stitch. Press the seam open. Join four more strips in the same way. Repeat for the remaining six strips.

1

2

2 Enlarge the tea cozy template by 200 percent. Lay the two pieces of patched fabric with right sides together. Place the template on top and draw around it with a fabric pen, then cut out the shape. Repeat to cut out the two pieces of lining and batting.

3 Place the lining with right sides together and lay one piece of batting on either side. Allowing a ½ in. (1 cm) seam, pin and then machine stitch along the sides and top curved edge. Trim the seams and press them open.
   Pin the patched fabric with right sides together and machine stitch a ½ in. (1 cm) seam along the sides and top curved edge. Trim the seams and press them open.

3

4 Slide the lining (with wrong sides—that is, the batting—together) inside the cover (with right sides together). Allowing a ½ in. (1 cm) seam, pin and then machine stitch along the bottom edge, leaving a 2½ in. (6 cm) gap through which to turn the cozy right sides out (in step 5). Press the seams open, then pull the lining back out of the cover (as shown below).

4

Tip

✿ Use similar weights and types of fabric—for example, cotton and cotton mixes—that can be washed at the same temperature to avoid shrinkage or color runs.

5

5 Pull the cozy through the gap in the bottom edge, so that the lining and cover are both right sides out (this will create an oval shape, with the lining making up one half and the cover the other half).

6 Take hold of the seam on both sides of what will be the bottom edge to open the cover and push the lining inside. Turn under the seam allowance at the gap and pin, then topstitch all around the bottom edge.

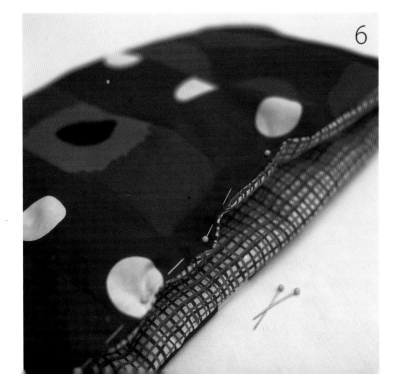

6

Decorative patch

1 Cut a 4 in. (10 cm) square of linen and fray the edges by pulling away a few threads.

Using the cup template, cut out one cup motif in the patterned fabric and glue it to the center of the linen patch. Outline the rim of the cup using a fabric pen, then draw around the saucer templates.

1

2 Using embroidery thread and the freehand embroidery foot on your sewing machine, follow the drawn lines and fill in the outside of the saucer with stitching.

Pin the patch on the front of the cozy. Using a needle and six strands of embroidery thread, sew it in place with running stitch (see pages 88–9). Catch only the top layer of fabric so that there are no stitches on the inside of the cozy.

2

Materials

For a standard four-cup coffeepot sleeve:

6 strips of fabric 6½ x 3½ in. (16 x 9 cm) for the outer cover

14½ x 6½ in. (37 x 16 cm) of fabric for the lining

Lightweight batting 14½ x 6½ in. (37 x 16 cm)

4¾ in. (12 cm) of Velcro

4 x 4 in. (10 x 10 cm) of linen for the patch

Scrap of fabric for the cup

Pins

Sewing thread

Sewing machine

Iron and ironing board

Pinking shears

Needle

Embroidery thread

Scissors

Fabric pen

Fabric glue

Coffeepot sleeve

1 Start by joining the strips of fabric together to make the outer cover. With right sides facing, pin along the long edge of two strips, allowing a ½ in. (1 cm) seam, and machine stitch. Press the seam open. Repeat until you have joined all six strips together.

3

1

3 Pin Velcro pieces centrally on each side edge (one on the front of the sleeve and one on the lining), then machine stitch.

Decorative patch

Follow the instructions as described for the tea cozy on page 99.

2 Cut out the lining and batting. Place the patched fabric and lining with right sides together. Lay the batting on top of the lining and pin the three fabrics together. Allowing a ½ in. (1 cm) seam, machine stitch around all four edges, leaving a 2 in. (5 cm) gap on one side edge.

Trim and press the seams open, then turn the fabric right sides out through the gap in the side seam. Turn the raw edges under at the gap and close with slip stitch (see step 2 on page 60).

2

Quilted patchwork bedspread

This pretty design is a simple introduction to the techniques of patchwork and quilting, using both hand-sewn and machine-stitched quilting techniques to make your own heirloom quilt. I used cotton fabric, but you could use silk for a more luxurious bedspread—if you do, make sure that you use silk thread for both machine stitching and hand sewing.

Materials

62 x 78 in. (158 x 198 cm) of white cotton for the center of the quilt

4 patches of white cotton 10 x 10 in. (25.5 x 25.5 cm) for the corners

7 patches of patterned fabric 10 x 10 in. (25.5 x 25.5 cm) for the side strips

7 patches of a second patterned fabric 10 x 10 in. (25.5 x 25.5 cm) for the side strips

17 patches of the first patterned fabric 5¾ x 10 in. (14.5 x 25.5 cm) for the top and bottom strips

17 patches of the second patterned fabric 5¾ x 10 in. (14.5 x 25.5 cm) for the top and bottom strips

94½ x 78½ in. (240 x 200 cm) of quilting batting

95¾ x 79¾ (243 x 203 cm) of cotton backing fabric

Tape measure

Dressmaking scissors

Pins

Sewing thread

Sewing machine

Iron and ironing board

Flower templates

Fabric pen

Tacking thread

Needle

Embroidery thread in three different colors

White or off-white quilting thread

TRACE OFF THE TEMPLATES, SHOWN HERE AT ACTUAL SIZE

1 Cut out all the patches, making sure you cut them all with the fabric running in the same direction.

To make up the side strips, place two contrasting patterned squares with right sides together and pin along one side, allowing a ⅝ in. (1.5 cm) seam, then machine stitch. Next, attach a contrasting patterned square to the first square in the same way. Repeat until you have joined seven alternating patterned squares in a line, then attach a white corner square to the first and last patterned squares. Make up the second strip in the same way. Press the seams open.

For the top and bottom strips of patchwork, take two rectangular patches, one of each pattern, and pin then stitch them together along one long edge, allowing a ⅝ in. (1.5 cm) seam as before. Continue alternating patterns until you have stitched 17 rectangles together per strip. Press the seams open.

1

3 Using the flower templates and a fabric pen, trace the motifs onto the four corner patches and in the center of the quilt. Start by tracing the largest template, then position the medium-sized template in the center of the motif and trace around that; repeat for the smallest template.

Scatter individual motifs randomly across the centerpiece of the fabric, intersecting some with the edge of the fabric so that only half or three-quarters of the flower is traced. Doing this helps prevent the design from looking too rigid.

2

2 Join the patchwork strips to the central fabric as follows. With right sides facing and allowing a ⅝ in. (1.5 cm) seam, pin one of the side strips (made up of square patches) to one side edge of the central fabric, matching up the edges and aligning the first and last patterned square with the corners of the central fabric. Machine stitch, then press the seam open. Join the opposite side strip in the same way.

Then join the top and bottom strips of patchwork (made up of rectangular patches) to the top and bottom edges of the central fabric. Join the sides of these strips to the white corner squares attached to the ends of the side strips. Press all the seams open.

3

4

6 Next, machine stitch around the edges of each patchwork square and rectangle on the machine to give a quilted look. (Match the color of the bobbin thread to the back fabric of your quilt and the color of the top thread to the top fabric of your quilt.)

Finish the edges by turning the edge of the top fabric over the batting so that it is encased. Then turn the 5/8 in. (1.5 cm) hem allowance of the backing fabric to the inside, so that it lies flat underneath the batting and lines up with the top edge of the quilt. Trim any excess fabric at the corners if necessary. Pin the layers together and topstitch using the machine around all four edges.

4 Lay the fabric right side down on the floor and smooth it flat. Place the batting on top and smooth it flat. Lay the backing fabric right side up on top of the batting, smoothing the fabric as before. Pin all three layers together and tack, as described in the second tip (see below right).

Using six strands of embroidery thread, work in running stitch (see pages 88–9) around the outline of the flower motifs on the four corner patches, using a different color for each flower.

5 Stitch the central flower motifs in the same way, using white or off-white quilting thread.

6

Tips

❀ You can use an ordinary foot for machine quilting, but loosen the thread tension so that the quilting can move easily under the foot.

❀ When quilting on the machine, it is essential to tack the layers of fabric together to prevent wrinkling. Sew tacking stitches horizontally and vertically across the quilt, starting at the center and working out in each direction. Finish by tacking two diagonal lines from corner to corner. While tacking, keep smoothing the fabric to keep it flat.

5

Sewing bag

Stash your sewing or knitting project, with needles and scissors, in this funky bag, and it's ready to take anywhere. There is a wide variety of bag handles available from specialty craft stores. I chose these for their retro feel, which works well with the patchwork fabric.

Materials

Selection of fabric sufficient for 31 patches for each side of the bag (I used 14 flower-patterned patches, 9 plain patches and 8 circle-patterned patches)

1 yard (1 m) of lining fabric

Bag handles

Hexagonal window template made from stiff card

Craft knife and cutting mat

Fabric pen

Dressmaking scissors

Thick backing or freezer paper for patches

Pins

Sticky tape

Needle

Tacking thread

Iron and ironing board

Sewing thread

Tape measure

Sewing machine

TRACE THE WINDOW TEMPLATE, SHOWN HERE AT ACTUAL SIZE

Tip

✂ When you have cut out all your patches and backed them with paper, separate them into groups, which you can then string together by threading through the patches with a needle and knotted thread. The patches can be pulled off easily as and when you need them when making up your patchwork.

1 Trace the hexagonal window template onto a piece of stiff card and cut it out using a craft knife. The outer edge of the template is the pattern for the fabric patches and includes a hem allowance; the inner edge is the pattern for the paper backing and is the size of the finished patch.

Lay the hexagonal window template on your fabric and, using the fabric pen, trace around the outer edge of the template. Make sure you lay the template in the same direction on the fabric for all the patches. Cut out the patches using dressmaking scissors.

Fold the backing paper over twice (so that you can cut out four shapes at once). Using the template again, trace around the inner edge of the hexagon, then carefully cut out 62 paper patches using a craft knife.

2 Back the fabric patches with the paper ones. To do this, lay the fabric patches right sides down on a flat surface and then pin a paper patch to the center of each. Fold the fabric edges over the paper backing one at a time and secure with a small piece of sticky tape.

Using a needle and tacking thread, tack round the edges, then remove the tape. Press the patches with an iron to give crisp edges.

3

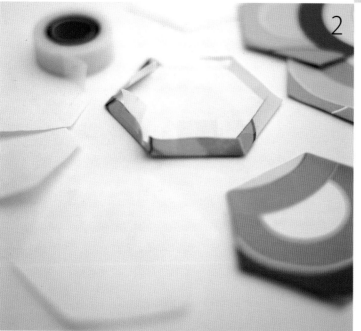

2

3 Starting with the central patch, join two hexagons together along one edge with overcast stitch. Place the patches with right sides together and, using a sharp threaded needle, pick up a few threads in the creased edge of both patches and pull through. Repeat neatly along the edge. (Try to avoid sewing the paper patches under the fabric, as this will make it easier to remove them and means the paper patches can be used again for another project.

Next, join a third hexagon to the sides of the first two patches in the same way, making sure that they are lined up. Continue joining hexagons around the edges of the first hexagon until you have attached patches to all six sides.

4 Continue working outward, tapering the patchwork so that it has a triangular shape—three patches wide at the top, five patches deep, and nine patches wide at the bottom—until you have used all 31 patches.

Remove the tacking, then lay the patchwork right side down on a flat surface and fold every other patch along the outer edges in half to create straight edges. Trim the paper backing of these patches to the folded line and trim the fabric to ½ in. (1 cm) away from the folded line.

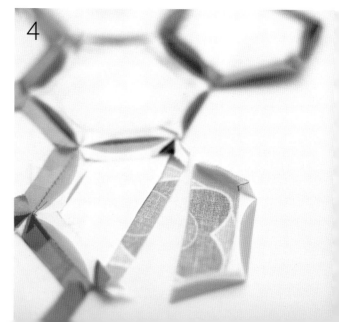

4

5 Working all around the edge of the piece of patchwork, fold the ½ in. (1 cm) of fabric over the edge of the paper and tack it in place. Then press the patches.

Repeat the above from step 3 to make up the other side of the bag.

Using one patchwork side of the bag as a template, cut out two pieces of lining fabric, adding ⅝ in. (1.5 cm) all around for the seams.

To make up the bag, place both patchwork pieces with right sides together and pin along the bottom edge of the bag. Measure 6 in. (15 cm) down one side from the top and pin from this point down the side to the bottom edge. Repeat for the other side of the bag.

Sew the pinned edges of the bag together with overcast stitch. Carefully remove the paper backing and press the bag. Turn right sides out.

6 Place the lining right sides together and, allowing a ⅝ in. (1.5 cm) seam, pin then machine stitch along the bottom edge and up the side edges, but stop sewing 6½ in. (16.5 cm) down from the top edge on both side seams.

Press the seams open, then press under a ⅝ in. (1.5 cm) seam allowance on the unstitched part of the side seams and along the top edge.

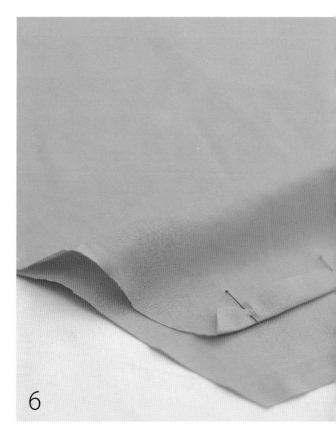

7 With the lining right sides together and the patchwork bag wrong sides together, slide the lining into the bag (with wrong sides of bag to wrong sides of lining).

Slide the top edges of the patchwork through the bag handles, neatly ruching the fabric if necessary so that it fits the shape. Pin and then tack on the inside to hold in place.

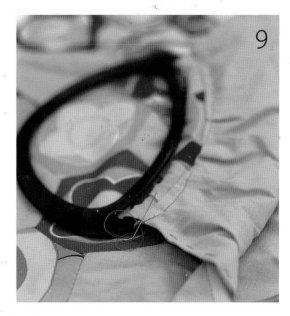

8 Line up the unstitched 6 in. (15 cm) of the side seams of the patchwork and lining, and pin them together. Then pin the folded-under top edge of the lining to the patchwork, just below the bag handle and covering the back of the patchwork to give a neat finish. Tack the sides and along the top of the lining. Topstitch using the machine along the width of the bag, just below the handle, to secure. Remove the tacking from the top edge and repeat to secure the other handle.

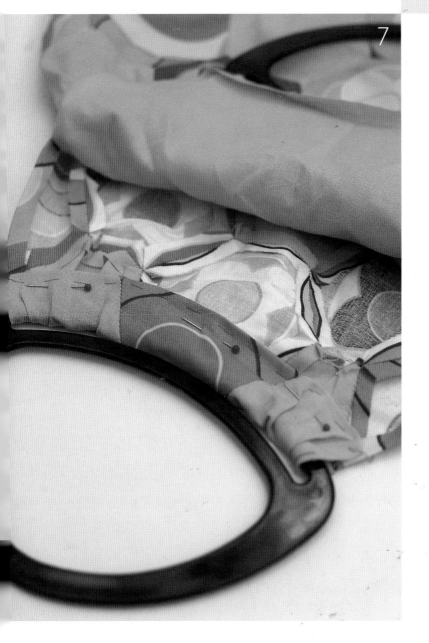

9 Using a needle and thread, slip stitch down the tacked side seams; remove the tacking.

Waterproof picnic rug

Keep this waterproof picnic rug in the trunk of your car and you'll always be ready for an impromptu feast at the beach or wherever you pull up when you're on the road. This project . combines rows of patchwork with strips of fabric that can all be easily stitched on the sewing machine. The rug is lined with batting for insulation and backed with tarp to make it waterproof. The handy ties on the back mean that you can roll it up neatly when it's not in use, making it ultra-practical.

Materials

45 patches of fabric 10 x 10 in. (25 x 25 cm)—including a ⅝ in. (1.5 cm) seam allowance

4 strips of fabric 10 x 79 in. (25 x 201 cm)—including a ⅝ in. (1.5 cm) seam allowance

2 x 2 yards (2 x 2 m) of batting

2 x 2 yards (2 x 2 m) of tarp material

9 yards (8.2 m) of bias binding

2 strips of fabric 4 x 39 in. (10 x 100 cm) for the ties

Dressmaking scissors

Tape measure

Pins

Sewing thread

Sewing machine

Iron and ironing board

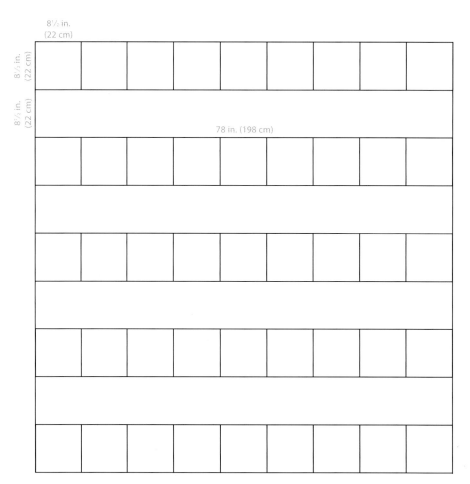

THE RUG IS MADE BY ALTERNATING ROWS OF PATCHWORK WITH SOLID STRIPS
FINISHED DIMENSIONS ARE APPROXIMATELY 2 x 2 yards (2 x 2m)

1 Cut the fabric to size. You need 45 square patches measuring 10 x 10 in. (25 x 25 cm) and four strips measuring 10 x 79 in. (25 x 201 cm).

Join nine patches together to create a long patchwork row. To do this, take the first two patches and, with right sides together and allowing a ⅝ in. (1.5 cm) seam, pin and then machine stitch along one edge of the patches. Join seven more patches in the same way. Repeat with the remaining patches to make five patchwork rows, arranging the fabric patches in the same order and direction in each row to give a uniform look to the finished piece. Press the seams open.

1

2

2 Stitch the patchwork rows to the fabric strips (see diagram on page 112). With right sides together and allowing a 1⅝ in. (1.5 cm) seam, pin along one long edge and then machine stitch. Repeat until all the pieces have been joined together, alternating the patchwork rows with the fabric strips. Press all the seams open.

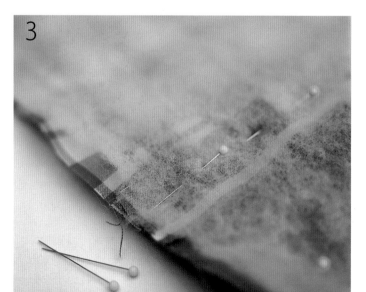

3

3 Cut the batting to size. If you need to use several pieces to make a 2 x 2 yard (2 x 2 m) square, overlap the pieces by about 1¼ in. (3 cm) and topstitch on the machine to join them. To attach the batting to the patchwork fabric, lay the fabric right side down, place the batting on top and smooth with your hands, then pin the layers together. Using the sewing machine, topstitch along the long seams that join the patchwork rows and the plain fabric strips together.

4 To make the ties, fold a 4 x 39 in. (10 x 100 cm) strip of fabric in half lengthwise with right sides together. Allowing a ⅝ in. (1.5 cm) seam, pin along one long edge and one end, and machine stitch. Press the seams open and turn the tie right sides out. Turn under the seam allowance at the open end and topstitch using the machine. Repeat for the other tie.

Cut the tarp to size and lay it flat on the floor, right side up. Measure 6 in. (15 cm) in from the top right corner and 6 in. (15 cm) down from the top edge, and mark with a pin. Repeat this process, measuring 14 in. (35 cm) in and 6 in. (15 cm) down from the top right corner, and mark with a pin. Measure 18 in. (45 cm) along one of the ties and mark with a pin. Line up this pin with the first pin on the tarp, and pin in place (removing the marker pin from the tarp). Working down toward the bottom of the rug, pin 4 in. (10 cm) more of the tie to the tarp backing. Repeat for the other tie, lining it up with the second marker pin on the tarp. Then machine stitch both ties in place, sewing along both long sides of the tie and across the ends to make a stitched rectangle shape.

5

4

5 Turn the tarp over, so that the wrong side is facing up, and lay the patchwork on top, right side up so that the batting is sandwiched between them. Pin the layers together. Starting in the middle of one edge, wrap the bias binding around the edge, enclosing all three layers of tarp backing, batting, and patchwork, then pin in place. Ease the bias binding around the corners, making them as neat as possible. When you reach the place where you started, overlap the bias binding slightly and turn the raw edge under, pin in place, and then machine stitch.

Patchwork basics

❀ If you are designing your own patchwork, it's best to draw it out on a piece of paper first. Do this by cutting the paper to a scaled-down version of your finished design—for example, 2 inches on paper could represent 1 foot of patchwork, or, using metric graph paper, a patchwork design of 2 x 2 meters can be drawn as a 20-cm square, so that the ratio is 1:10.

❀ Draw your design using colored pencils. Try to match the colors to each of the fabrics you want to use, as this will help you check that the pattern works. To start with, stick to two or three different colored or patterned fabrics, so that things don't get overly complicated.

❀ To work out roughly how much of each fabric you will need, take the measurements of the design as though you were making it in one piece and add an extra 36–39 in. (90–100 cm) for seams. Then divide this total proportionally according to the colors you are using—for example, light blue 20 percent, deep blue 60 percent and white 20 percent.

❀ For inspiration and guidance on how to place patches and on how to use color and pattern to graphic effect in your patchwork, it's worth looking at old designs. The single most important thing is for each patch to be clearly defined—this will enable you to "read" the pattern, whereas if the colors all meld together, the pattern will be lost, defeating the purpose of patchwork. Definition can be achieved by a change of tone—say, aqua against sky blue—or by using contrasting colors—such as red next to yellow. Another effective way of achieving this is by juxtaposing different textures—cut-pile velvet against stiff linen, for example— or patterns—a ditzy all-over floral print contrasted with a woven damask and checked fabric can look especially striking.

Color can also be used to give a three-dimensional effect. For example, square colored patches stitched onto a black background to build up a cube-shaped pattern, where two sides are colored and one is black to create a silhouette, produces an optical illusion of depth.

Printed fabric can be applied so as to create a sense of distance and impart a dynamic quality to the design of a quilt. Start by using the smallest prints for patches in the center, gradually increasing the scale of prints as you work out to the borders, where patches cut from the largest, boldest prints should be used. When choosing printed fabric for patchwork, make sure that the design is not so large that when you cut out your patches the pattern disappears and becomes meaningless.

Printed fabric can also be cut so that the pattern creates its own design. Try cutting your patch with the print in the center to make a rosette or abstract motif. Diamond or triangular patches can be cut so that the main part of the pattern is located at the angles, so that when all the patches are stitched together they will make new patterns of their own. Stripes can be used in this way, too, and are also particularly good for creating optical effects.

6 TIPS for perfect patches

1 It is crucial to cut out patches carefully so that they are a uniform shape and will fit together well.

2 Choose fabrics of the same weight, so that the pieces will lie flat.

3 Use a template to cut out your fabric—it should be ¼ in. (6 mm) bigger all around than your finished patch. These can be homemade from stiff card or metal, while plastic templates are available from most craft stores.

4 Back the fabric patches with paper—this will help make a neat patch with sharp edges, which makes it much easier to join them together. Remove the paper backings when the patchwork is complete. (See pages 106–9.)

5 Make sure the grain of the fabric and direction of the print lie the same way for each patch.

6 Use a window template. These are either an empty frame, where the outer edge is the size of the patch including seam allowance and the inner edge is the size of the finished patch, or a piece of clear plastic that you can use to frame up patterned fabrics, ensuring perfect positioning before cutting.

The three patchwork stars shown opposite illustrate how the same design can look completely different depending on your choice of fabric. In the case of the blue and white patchwork star (top right), it is the change in pattern from stripes to floral that picks out the star design. Contrasting a brightly colored patterned fabric with a plain fabric gives the green patchwork star (bottom left) a bold, almost three-dimensional, effect. White linen is contrasted with creamy textured fabric to give the white patchwork star (bottom right) a much more subtle look.

Make it new

Just because a favorite summer dress is a little faded or the curtains from your childhood bedroom are a bit worn at the edges, there's no need to part with them. The popularity for all things vintage means that it's cool to reuse something old to make something new, especially if the item in question is something you cherish, reminds you of good times, or is a part of family history. It's all about looking at things in a different light and spotting their potential. A pair of chintz curtains can be cut down and used to reupholster the chair in your home office. Your grandmother's fine linen napkins and embroidered placemats can be pieced together to make exquisite pillowcases or table runners. Try sewing together a long-forgotten selection of psychedelic neckties to make a groovy bag, or cut up that patchy, sun-bleached candlewick bedspread or kitsch Fifties silk scarf to make sumptuous cushion covers.

Silk-scarf bolster

Decorate a daybed or sofa with a collection of bolsters made from vintage silk scarves. You can find old scarves in secondhand shops or on Internet websites such as eBay; alternatively, rummage through your grandma's closet— with her permission, of course—and see what you turn up.

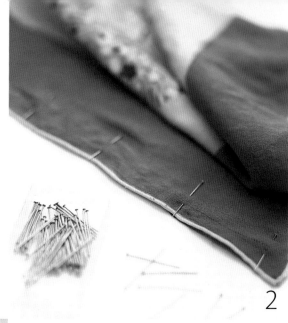

2

Materials

Square silk scarf, approximately 34 x 34 in. (86 x 86 cm)

Bolster cushion, 20 in. (50 cm) long, 8 in. (20 cm) in diameter

24 in. (60 cm) of 1 in.- (25 mm-) wide ribbon

Tape measure

Dressmaking scissors

Sewing thread

Sewing machine

Pins

Iron and ironing board

1

2 Fold the silk scarf in half with right sides together and pin along the longest edge, allowing a ½ in. (1 cm) seam. Machine stitch along this seam using running stitch to make a tube-shaped cover for the bolster. Press the seam open.

3 Turn the cover right side out and slide the bolster cushion into the cover. Cut the ribbon in half, cutting on the slant to prevent the ends from fraying. Bunch the fabric together at both ends of the cushion and secure by tying the ribbon in a bow.

3

1 Measure the circumference of the bolster cushion and add ¾ in. (2 cm) to this measurement. Cut along one edge of the silk scarf to this measurement. Using the fabric rolling foot on your sewing machine, stitch along the cut edge to prevent the fabric from fraying and to give a neat finish.

Caftan shoe bag

This is a good way of using vintage clothing or old clothes that aren't in good enough condition to wear but are still pretty; antique nightdresses and slips also work well. The key to this project is to pick an area on the clothing that has plenty of detail, such as a beaded neckline, gathered pleats around a waistband, a row of buttons on the back of a dress, or an embroidered cuff. This basic design can be adapted to make a larger bag for delicate underwear or a smaller pouch for jewelry.

Materials

Dress, skirt or top

36 x 16 in. (90 x 40 cm) of lining fabric

1½ yards (1.5 m) of ¼ in.- (5 mm-) wide ribbon

Tape measure

Dressmaking scissors

Pins

Sewing thread

Sewing machine

Iron and ironing board

Safety pins

1 Examine your piece of clothing and work out which part of it you would like to be the focal point of your shoe bag. I wanted the sequinned neckline of this caftan to be on the front of my shoe bag. Cut two pieces of fabric from your clothing, each measuring 17 x 13 in. (43 x 33 cm).

Cut out one piece of lining fabric measuring 33 x 13 in. (83 x 33 cm). Fold it in half lengthwise, with right sides together. Allowing a ⅝ in. (1.5 cm) seam, pin, then machine stitch both long sides together. Press the seams open.

3 Slide the lining (with right sides together) inside the bag (with wrong sides together). Make sure that the seam allowance at the top edges of both parts of the bag is turned inside and then line up the top edges of the bag and lining. Pin and then topstitch using the sewing machine. Press the seam to give a neat finish.

2 Lay the two pieces of your main fabric with right sides together. Allowing a ⅝ in. (1.5 cm) seam, pin and then machine stitch along the bottom edge and 13¼ in. (33.5 cm) up both side edges. Leave a ⅝ in. (1.5 cm) gap on both side edges and then stitch the remainder of the side seams (the gap is to create the channel for the drawstring).

Press the seams open. Turn the top edges of both the lining and the outer bag over by ⅝ in. (1.5 cm) and press flat. Turn the outer bag right sides out.

4

4 Next, create the drawstring channel. Starting at the top of the gap in one side seam, stitch a line all the way around the width of the bag, finishing back at the place where you started. Repeat, starting at the lower edge of the same gap and again finishing where you started.

Tips

✂ You can also make the bag wider and longer to hold footwear such as boots, or make it smaller for lightweight shoes such as thongs or ballet-style pumps.

✂ If you are using a V-shaped neckline for the front of your bag, cut another piece of cloth from the same garment and use it to fill in the V shape so you have a solid piece of fabric.

5

5 Cut the length of ribbon in half and attach a safety pin to the end of one piece. Insert the safety pin into the hole in the left side seam and thread the ribbon all the way through the channel, finishing where you started. Remove the safety pin and tie the ends of the ribbon together. Repeat with the other piece of ribbon, but start threading it through the hole in the right side seam.

Retro curtain floor cushions

The fabric used for these cushions was found buried beneath a pile of musty chintz curtains in a rather unpromising-looking junk store in a small rural village on the Welsh borders, which just goes to show that anywhere you happen to be passing is worth investigating. While covering an entire sofa in these swinging prints might be a bit overwhelming, a scattering of floor cushions will inject a fun-filled blast of color to any living room.

Materials

20 x 20 x 4 in. (50 x 50 x 10 cm) cushion pad

2 pieces of fabric 21 x 21 in. (53 x 53 cm) for the top and bottom pieces of the cover

5 x 21 in. (13 x 53 cm) strip of fabric for the front gusset

2 strips of fabric 5 x 19 in. (13 x 48 cm) for the side gussets

2 strips of fabric 3 x 23 in. (8 x 58 cm) for the back gusset

20 in. (50 cm) zipper

Pinking shears

Pins

Sewing thread

Sewing machine

Needle

Tacking thread

Iron and ironing board

1 Cut out all the fabric pieces, then insert the zipper into the back gusset. To do this, place the two 3 x 23 in. (8 x 58 cm) fabric strips with right sides together and pin along one long edge allowing a ⅝ in. (1.5 cm) seam. Machine stitch 1¾ in. (4 cm) in from each end, leaving a 20 in. (50 cm) opening for the zipper. Tack the opening together along the seam and then press the seam open. Remove the tacking and pin the zipper in place.

2 Tack the zipper in position. Then, using the zipper foot on your sewing machine, sew as close to the zipper as possible. Remove the tacking and open the zipper.

3 With a ⅝ in. (1.5 cm) seam, pin one end of each side gusset to either end of the zipped gusset. Machine stitch, leaving ⅝ in. (1.5 cm) unsewn at both ends of the seams so that the top and bottom of the cover can be attached.

Pin and machine stitch the front gusset to the side gussets, again leaving ⅝ in. (1.5 cm) unsewn at both ends of the seams.

4

Tips

✂ Pipe the edges of your cushion to give it a more structured look, adding the piping at steps 4 and 5 when you join the gusset to the top and bottom pieces of the cushion cover. Piping can be made in fabric that matches your cover or in a contrasting fabric that will highlight the cushion's shape.

✂ To make your own piping, cut strips of fabric on the bias (diagonally across the grain) and machine stitch the strips together. Cutting fabric on the bias makes it more flexible and easier to work around corners and curves. Next, stitch the strips around piping cord, using the zipper foot on the sewing machine.

4 Close the zipper. With right sides together and allowing a ⅝ in. (1.5 cm) seam, pin and then tack the top piece of the cushion cover to the top edge of the gusset. Make sure that the corners match, then machine stitch. Remove the tacking, trim the corners and seam allowances, and press the seams open.

5 Open the zipper and attach the bottom piece of the cushion cover to the lower edge of the gusset in the same way. Trim the seam allowances and corners and press the seams open.

Turn the cushion cover right side out through the zipper opening and press the fabric again, then insert the cushion pad and close the zipper.

5

Vintage doily curtain panel

It's quite easy to amass a collection of vintage lace doilies. Charity stores and junk stores often have piles or baskets of them and box lots at auctions are well worth a look, too. Here the doilies are stitched onto a muslin panel, which lets the light shine through, highlighting the fine detail, but still giving privacy when hung at a window.

Materials

Muslin or voile curtain panel

Selection of doilies

Iron and ironing board

Pins

Needle

Sewing thread

Sewing machine

Scissors

1 Start by ironing all your doilies and the curtain panel. Then lay the curtain panel flat on the floor or on a large table and arrange the doilies on it.

Tips

❉ If all your doilies are made of cotton or linen, you could try dyeing them—use hand dye rather than machine dye, as a spin cycle will be too vigorous and may ruin them.

❉ To whiten yellowed doilies, try soaking them in a solution of two tablespoons of borax (available from pharmacies) dissolved in a liter of warm water (this will remove vegetable stains from fabric, too). Alternatively, soak them in diluted bleach and rinse well.

2

2 Pin the doilies in place. Depending on how delicate they are, you may have to use a combination of machine stitching and hand-sewing to attach them to the curtain panel. Ultra-fine lacy doilies are best attached by hand using overcast stitch (see step 3 on page 108), while less fine pieces can be attached using the sewing machine. If you are using the machine, match the color of the top thread to the doily and the color of the bobbin thread to the curtain panel.

Tea-towel laundry bag

Cotton or linen tea towels are perfect for making into a laundry bag, as the material is hardwearing and easy to wash. Hang this large bag on the back of a door and there's no excuse for leaving your dirty clothes scattered on the floor. You could make several bags—one each for white, colored, and dark washes, or one for each member of your household. The cross-stitch motif adds a subtle touch of decoration and could be different for each bag to personalize them.

Materials

Selection of tea towels

Tape measure

Dressmaking scissors

Pins

Sewing thread

Sewing machine

Iron and ironing board

Square of waste canvas

Needle

Tacking thread

Embroidery thread

Water spray

Tweezers

1 Start by cutting six strips from your tea towels, each one measuring 26 x 8¼ in. (65 x 21 cm). Place two strips with right sides together. Allowing a ⅝ in. (1.5 cm) seam, pin and then machine stitch along one long edge of the strips. Attach a third strip in the same way to make a single piece of fabric measuring 26 x 22½ (65 x 57 cm). Repeat to join the other three strips together to create a second piece of fabric. Press the seams open.

To make up the bag, place the two pieces of fabric with right sides together and, allowing a ⅝ in. (1.5 cm) seam, pin along the bottom edge of the bag and up both sides. Machine stitch, then press the seams open.

Turn the top edge of the bag over twice to conceal the raw edges, pin in place, then machine stitch. Press to give a neat finish, then turn the bag right side out.

2 To make the handles, cut long strips 4 in. (10 cm) wide from the remaining tea towels. Join them together, end to end, to make a strip 32 in. (80 cm) long. Fold the strip in half lengthwise with right sides together. Allowing a ⅝ in. (1.5 cm) seam, pin along the long edge and one end, then machine stitch. Press the seams open and turn right sides out. Turn the raw edges under by ⅝ in. (1.5 cm) at the open end and pin it closed. Repeat for the second handle.

Attach the handles to the outside of the bag. To do this, pin both ends of one strip to the front of the bag, 6 in. (15 cm) in from each side and 1¾ in. (4 cm) down from the top edge. Using the sewing machine, topstitch the handle securely in place. Repeat to attach the second handle to the back of the bag.

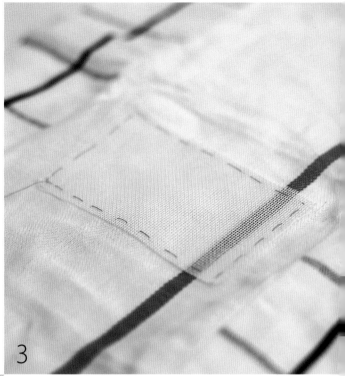

3

2

3 Cut a piece of waste canvas measuring 4 x 8 in. (10 x 20 cm) and position it centrally on the front of the bag, 8 in. (20 cm) down from the top edge. Pin and then tack the waste canvas onto the bag.

4 Using a needle and two strands of embroidery thread, cross-stitch the heart and birds motif onto the bag following the chart below (a square on the chart represents a block of four on the canvas). Start in the center of the design and work outward. To make a cross-stitch, bring the needle up through both layers of fabric (make sure that you don't split the threads on the waste canvas, as this will make it difficult to remove) then back down through a hole diagonally opposite the one you came up through; pull the thread through. Bring the needle up through a hole directly below the one you just pulled the thread through then back down through the hole directly opposite, making an "X" shape. Repeat to fill the design.

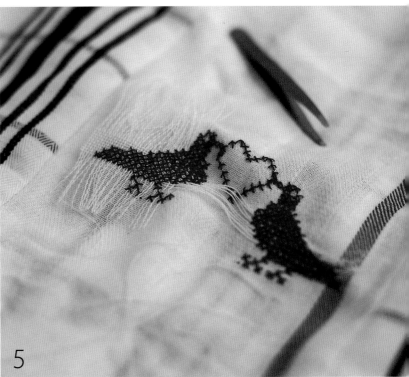

5

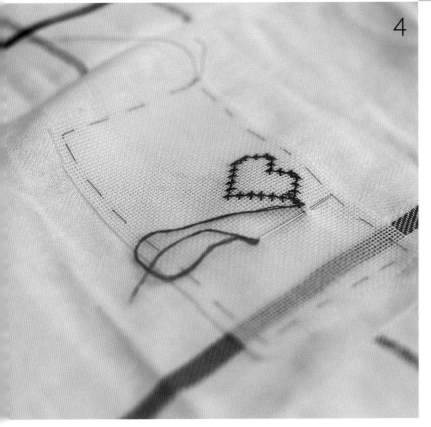

4

5 When you have finished the embroidery, spray the waste canvas with water to soften it. Remove the tacking thread and, using a pair of tweezers, carefully pull out each warp and weft thread of the waste canvas. Finally, press the design from the back.

ONE CROSS-STITCH IS EQUAL TO A BLOCK OF FOUR SQUARES
ON THE WASTE CANVAS WITH 17/18 THREADS PER INCH

Vintage patterns

What is a vintage fabric? Strictly speaking, it's any fabric that's old, but the really hot stuff to look out for is fabric from the Forties, Fifties, Sixties and Seventies—the Roaring Twenties, the Thirties, and even the Disco Eighties are enjoying a fashion revival, too. If you're trying to source vintage or retro fabrics, don't limit yourself to fabric on a roll, as this is increasingly hard to find—many companies are reissuing popular designs from these eras, so you can often buy old designs new. Scour junk stores, sale rooms and the Internet for home-furnishing items such as bedlinen, tea towels, curtains, tablecloths, and napkins as an alternative source of vintage fabrics that you can cut up and make into something else.

Project ideas and themes

❀ Napkins from any era can easily be made into covers for throw pillows—just cut them down to size, or piece a few together if they are small, add a square of plain fabric to make up the back (follow the instructions on pages 94–5), and arrange them in groups on your sofa and armchairs.

❀ A retro tablecloth can be used to make a wall hanging or backed with tarp to transform it into a travel rug for picnics (see page 115 for details on how to back fabric with tarp). Look out for super-graphic prints in flat, bold colors from the Sixties; designs by the Finnish company Marimekko are highly collectable.

❀ Printed linen tea towels can be made up into floor cushions for a playroom or used to cover seat pads for outdoor furniture (see pages 128–31). Colorful Fifties designs are delightfully kitsch and a good choice. Try to collect designs linked by a certain color or visual theme, such as food or kitchen motifs.

❀ Mix and match floral fabrics, patching together vintage finds with bold contemporary prints. The key to making this look work is to contrast different scales of pattern and then mix in the odd bit of plain fabric to give all those blooms some breathing space.

❀ Don't just look for fabric—keep your eyes peeled for retro sewing patterns and craft magazines, too. They're packed with projects and patterns, but by far the best thing about them is the photography and illustrations, which are often inspiring as well as highly amusing (especially issues from the Sixties and Seventies) and excellent documents of design history.

❀ Really small scraps of fabric can be used to make pincushions. Fashion them into small creatures, stitching on eyes, nose, and ears, or just make simple pillow shapes and decorate them with a bow.

❀ As little as 20 in. (50 cm) of fabric is enough to make a cushion cover, but there's no need to make regular-shaped cushions. Instead, take inspiration for the cushion's shape from the design on the fabric—for example, atomic-inspired prints from the Fifties reflected the angular design of much of the era's furniture, as well as the developments that were occurring in science and space travel, so triangular or geometric forms work well with these patterns. To make your own pad, simply take a pattern from the cover you have made and make it up in lining fabric. To stuff it, you can either pull apart an old cushion or pillow, or buy some synthetic filling.

❀ For a piece of instant no-sew artwork, stretch a cast-off of fabric over a canvas frame and secure it on the back with a staple gun—the bigger the canvas, the bigger impact it will have when you hang it on your wall. Large-scale psychedelic and flower-power prints are particularly well-suited to this idea.

Index

Main references to stitches are indicated in **bold** type.

Acknowledgments

My warmest thanks to all the people who have contributed to this book for all their hard work and enthusiasm, especially Zia Mattocks, who somehow gets her head around all the sewing techniques and keeps us all on track; Maggie Town for great design and art direction; and Chris Tubbs for his beautiful images, calm patience, and for taking more pictures in a day than I ever thought humanly possible. And, of course, thanks to my family for their continual support and encouragement, particularly Andy, with a special "big up" to Grandma and Grandpa for babysitting services during the photoshoot. Thanks, too, go to Jacqui Small for making it all possible.